Walt Disney's Donald Duck in Froggy Fortune

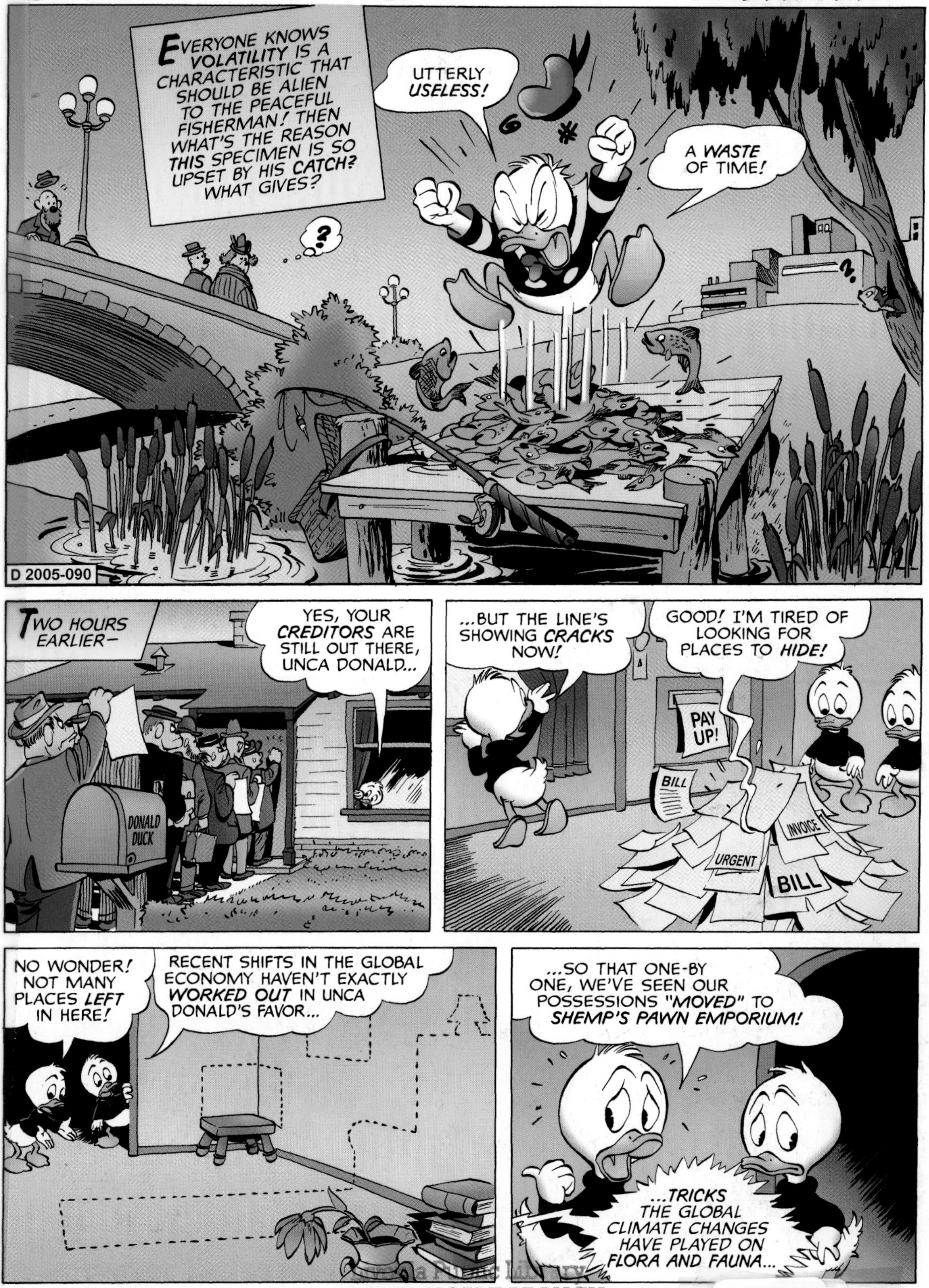
EVERYONE KNOWS VOLATILITY IS A CHARACTERISTIC THAT SHOULD BE ALIEN TO THE PEACEFUL FISHERMAN! THEN WHAT'S THE REASON THIS SPECIMEN IS SO UPSET BY HIS CATCH? WHAT GIVES?
UTTERLY USELESS!
A WASTE OF TIME!
?
D 2005-090
TWO HOURS EARLIER—
YES, YOUR CREDITORS ARE STILL OUT THERE, UNCA DONALD...
DONALD DUCK
...BUT THE LINE'S SHOWING CRACKS NOW!
GOOD! I'M TIRED OF LOOKING FOR PLACES TO HIDE!
PAY UP!
BILL
INVOICE
URGENT
BILL
NO WONDER! NOT MANY PLACES LEFT IN HERE!
RECENT SHIFTS IN THE GLOBAL ECONOMY HAVEN'T EXACTLY WORKED OUT IN UNCA DONALD'S FAVOR...
...SO THAT ONE-BY ONE, WE'VE SEEN OUR POSSESSIONS "MOVED" TO SHEMP'S PAWN EMPORIUM!
...TRICKS THE GLOBAL CLIMATE CHANGES HAVE PLAYED ON FLORA AND FAUNA...

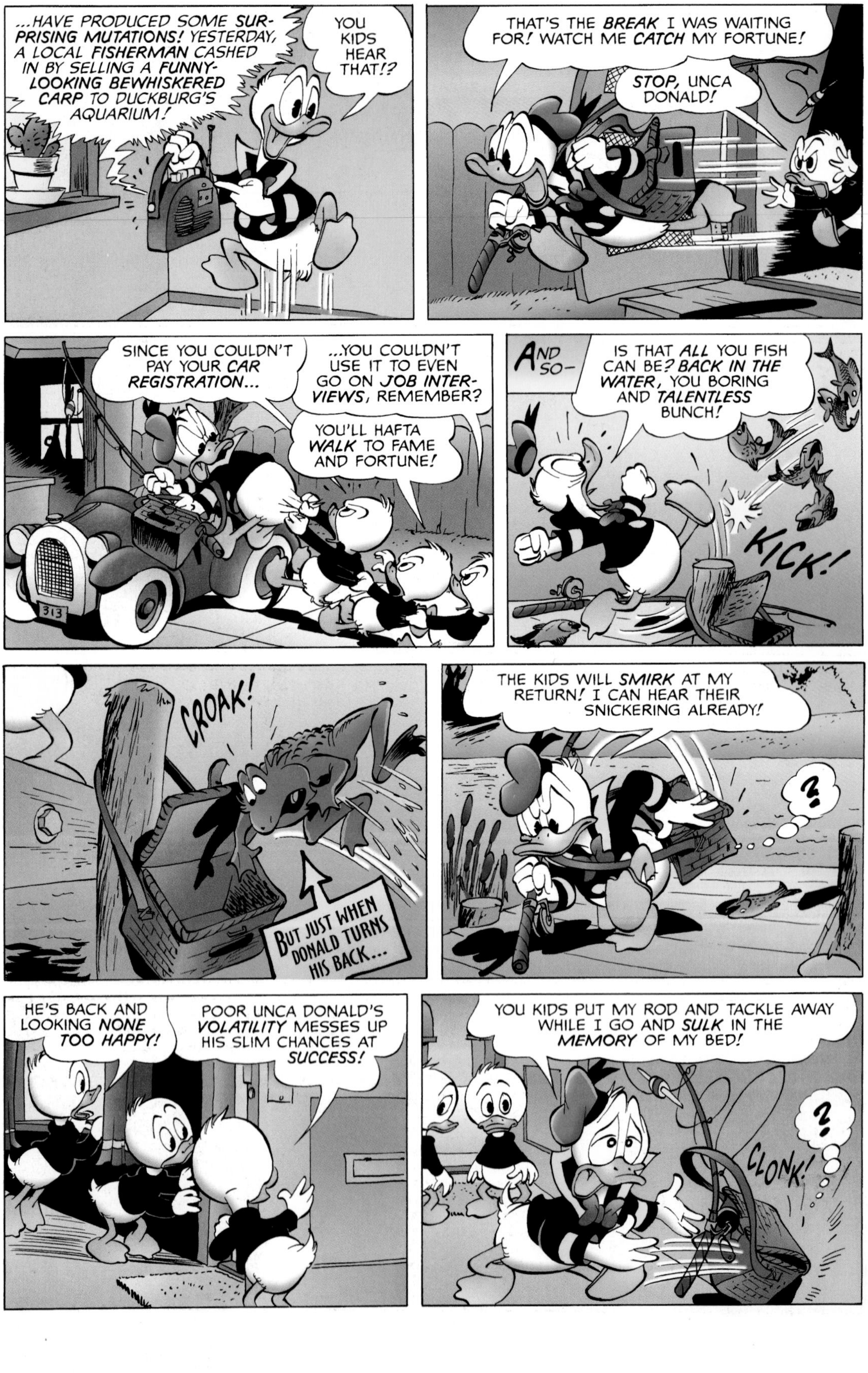
...HAVE PRODUCED SOME SURPRISING MUTATIONS! YESTERDAY, A LOCAL FISHERMAN CASHED IN BY SELLING A FUNNY-LOOKING BEWHISKERED CARP TO DUCKBURG'S AQUARIUM!
YOU KIDS HEAR THAT!?
THAT'S THE BREAK I WAS WAITING FOR! WATCH ME CATCH MY FORTUNE!
STOP, UNCA DONALD!
SINCE YOU COULDN'T PAY YOUR CAR REGISTRATION...
...YOU COULDN'T USE IT TO EVEN GO ON JOB INTERVIEWS, REMEMBER?
YOU'LL HAFTA WALK TO FAME AND FORTUNE!
313
AND SO—
IS THAT ALL YOU FISH CAN BE? BACK IN THE WATER, YOU BORING AND TALENTLESS BUNCH!
KICK!
CROAK!
BUT JUST WHEN DONALD TURNS HIS BACK...
THE KIDS WILL SMIRK AT MY RETURN! I CAN HEAR THEIR SNICKERING ALREADY!
?
HE'S BACK AND LOOKING NONE TOO HAPPY!
POOR UNCA DONALD'S VOLATILITY MESSES UP HIS SLIM CHANCES AT SUCCESS!
YOU KIDS PUT MY ROD AND TACKLE AWAY WHILE I GO AND SULK IN THE MEMORY OF MY BED!
?
CLONK!

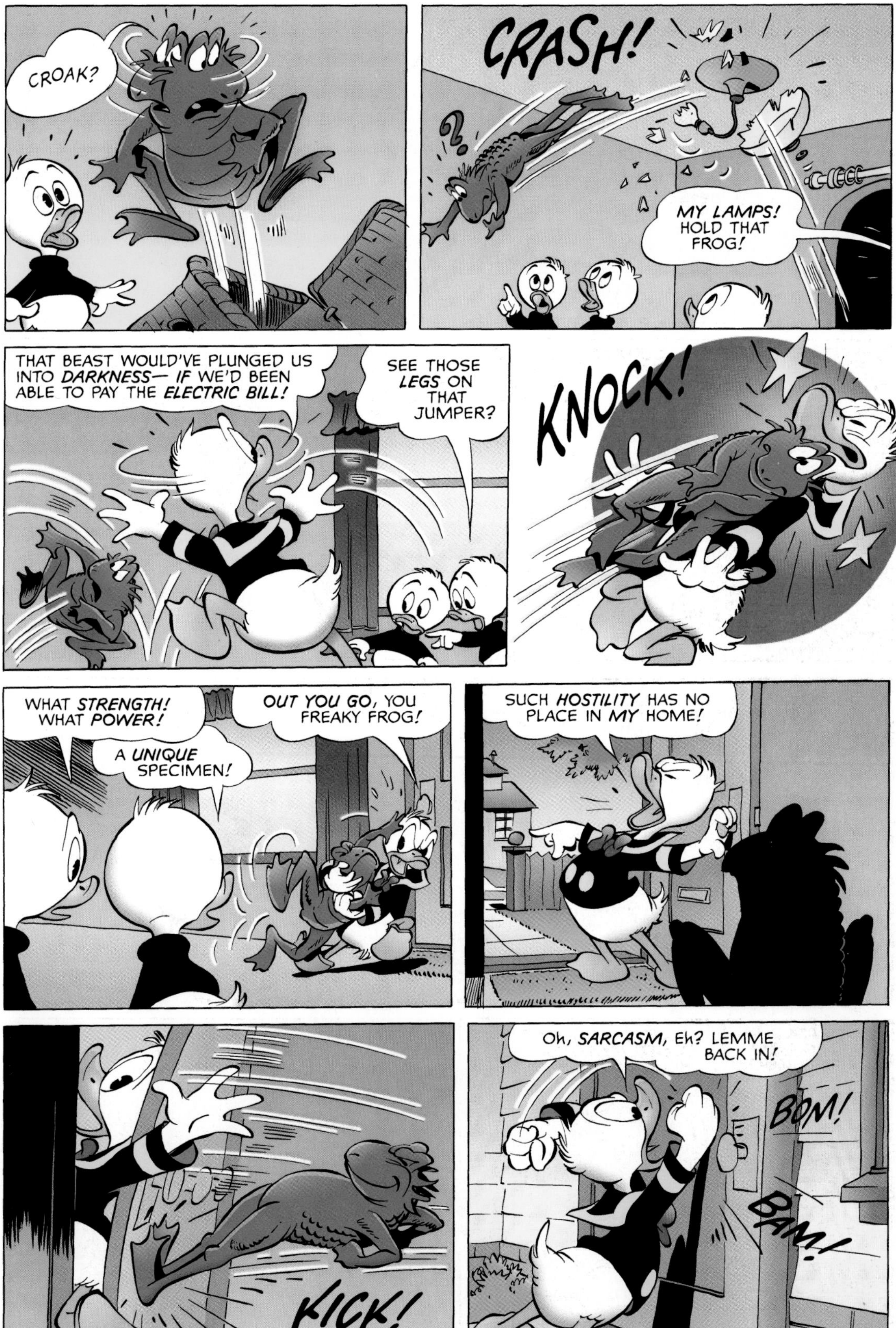
CROAK?
CRASH!
?
MY LAMPS! HOLD THAT FROG!
THAT BEAST WOULD'VE PLUNGED US INTO DARKNESS— IF WE'D BEEN ABLE TO PAY THE ELECTRIC BILL!
SEE THOSE LEGS ON THAT JUMPER?
KNOCK!
WHAT STRENGTH! WHAT POWER!
A UNIQUE SPECIMEN!
OUT YOU GO, YOU FREAKY FROG!
SUCH HOSTILITY HAS NO PLACE IN MY HOME!
KICK!
Oh, SARCASM, Eh? LEMME BACK IN!
BOM!
BAM!

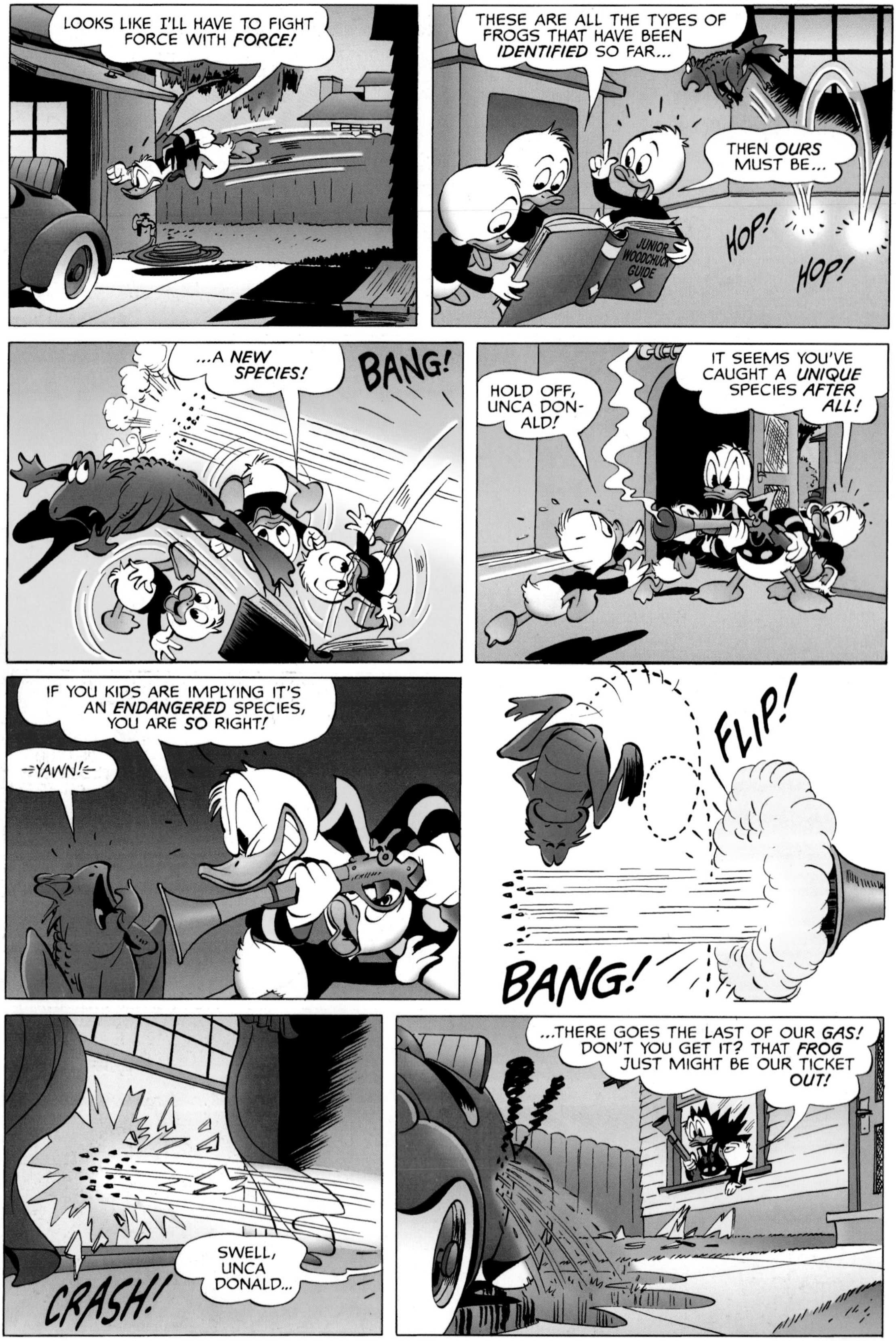

LOOKS LIKE I'LL HAVE TO FIGHT FORCE WITH FORCE!
THESE ARE ALL THE TYPES OF FROGS THAT HAVE BEEN IDENTIFIED SO FAR...
THEN OURS MUST BE...
JUNIOR WOODCHUCK GUIDE
HOP!
HOP!
...A NEW SPECIES!
BANG!
HOLD OFF, UNCA DONALD!
IT SEEMS YOU'VE CAUGHT A UNIQUE SPECIES AFTER ALL!
IF YOU KIDS ARE IMPLYING IT'S AN ENDANGERED SPECIES, YOU ARE SO RIGHT!
YAWN!
FLIP!
BANG!
SWELL, UNCA DONALD...
CRASH!
...THERE GOES THE LAST OF OUR GAS! DON'T YOU GET IT? THAT FROG JUST MIGHT BE OUR TICKET OUT!

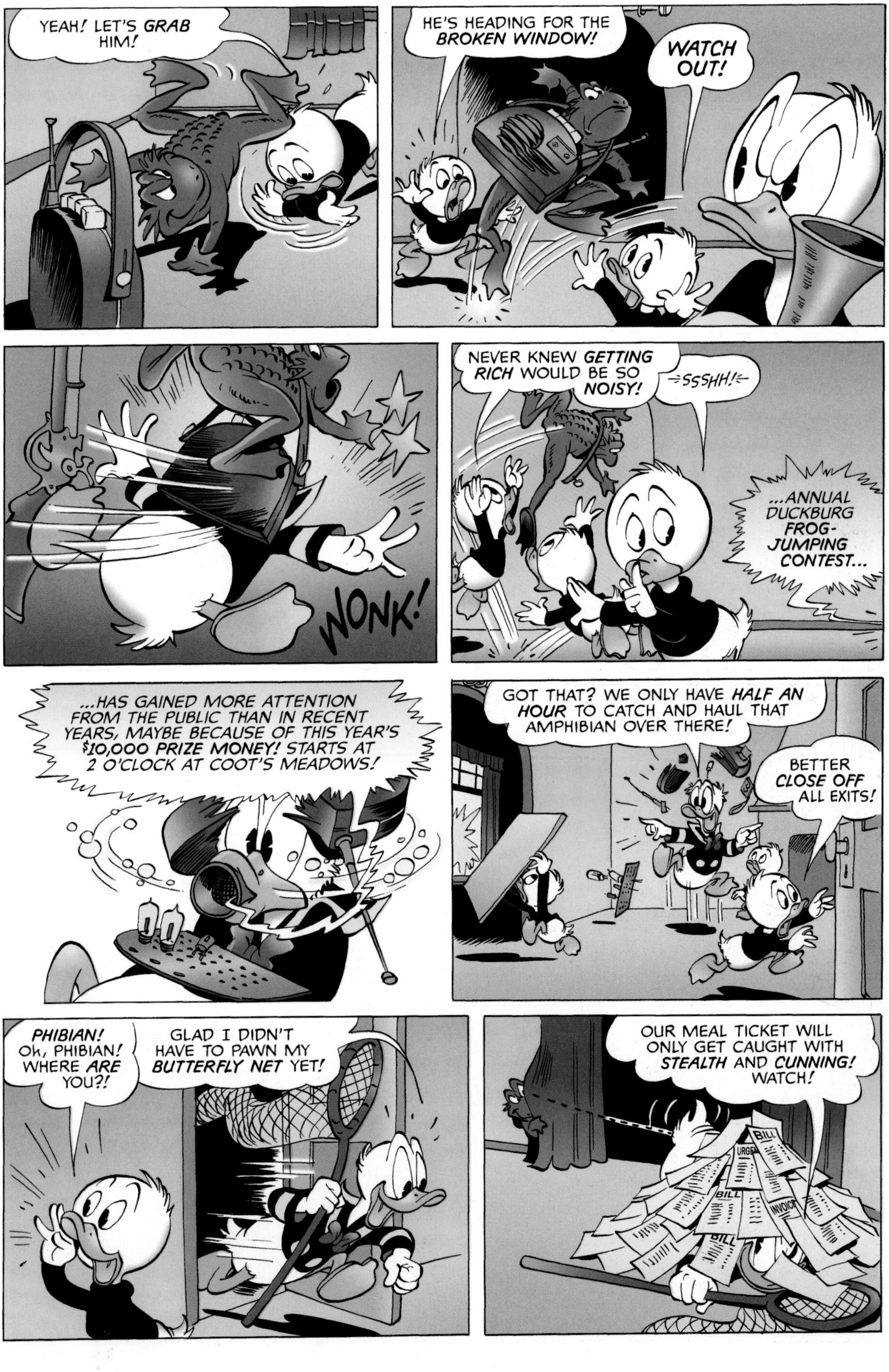
YEAH! LET'S GRAB HIM!
HE'S HEADING FOR THE BROKEN WINDOW!
WATCH OUT!
WONK!
NEVER KNEW GETTING RICH WOULD BE SO NOISY!
SSSHH!
...ANNUAL DUCKBURG FROG-JUMPING CONTEST...
...HAS GAINED MORE ATTENTION FROM THE PUBLIC THAN IN RECENT YEARS, MAYBE BECAUSE OF THIS YEAR'S $10,000 PRIZE MONEY! STARTS AT 2 O'CLOCK AT COOT'S MEADOWS!
GOT THAT? WE ONLY HAVE HALF AN HOUR TO CATCH AND HAUL THAT AMPHIBIAN OVER THERE!
BETTER CLOSE OFF ALL EXITS!
PHIBIAN! Oh, PHIBIAN! WHERE ARE YOU?!
GLAD I DIDN'T HAVE TO PAWN MY BUTTERFLY NET YET!
OUR MEAL TICKET WILL ONLY GET CAUGHT WITH STEALTH AND CUNNING! WATCH!
BILL
URGE
BILL
INVOIC
BILL

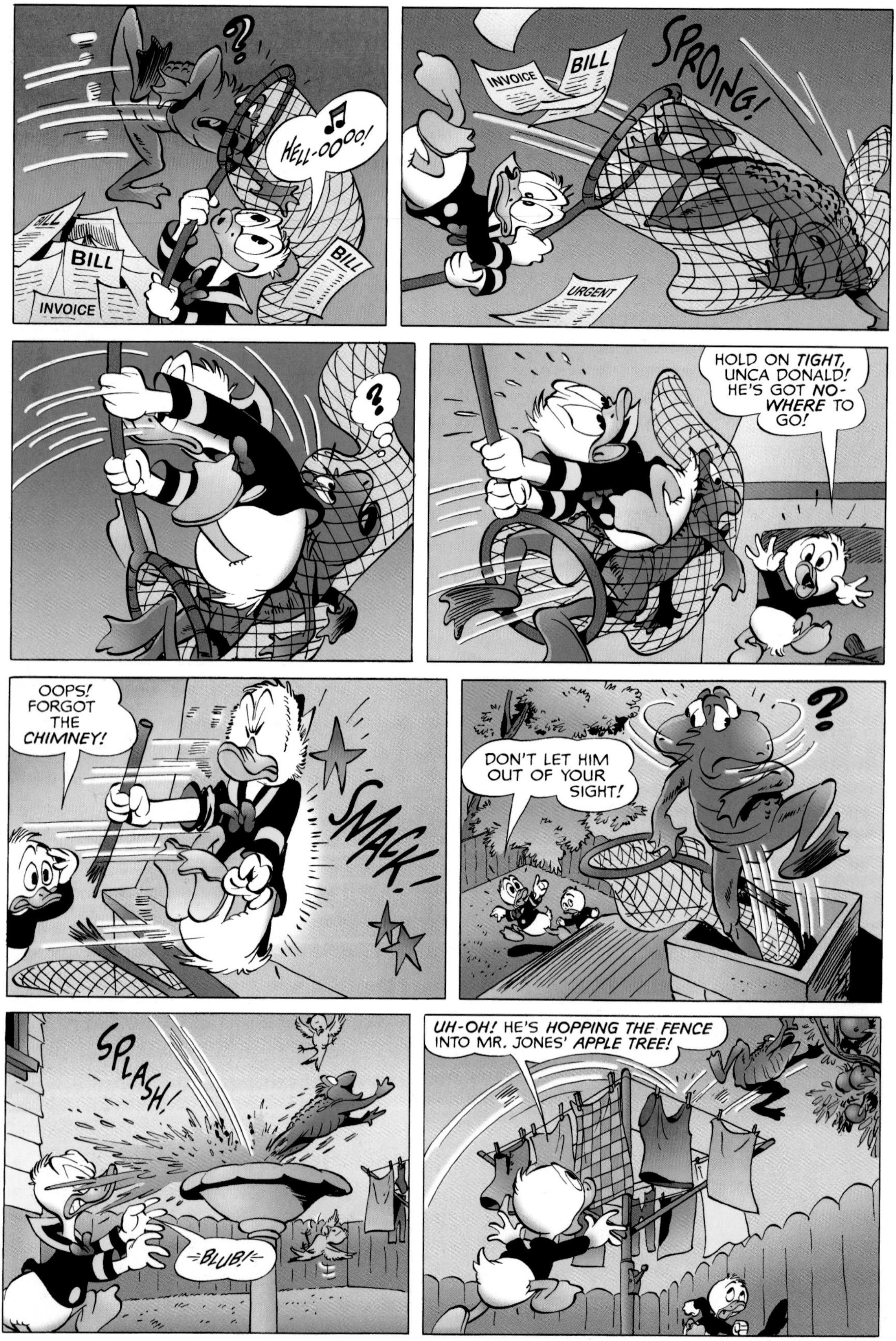
BILL
BILL
INVOICE
BILL
HELL-OOOO!
INVOICE
BILL
SPROING!
URGENT
HOLD ON TIGHT, UNCA DONALD! HE'S GOT NO-WHERE TO GO!
OOPS! FORGOT THE CHIMNEY!
SMACK!
DON'T LET HIM OUT OF YOUR SIGHT!
SPLASH!
BLUB!
UH-OH! HE'S HOPPING THE FENCE INTO MR. JONES' APPLE TREE!

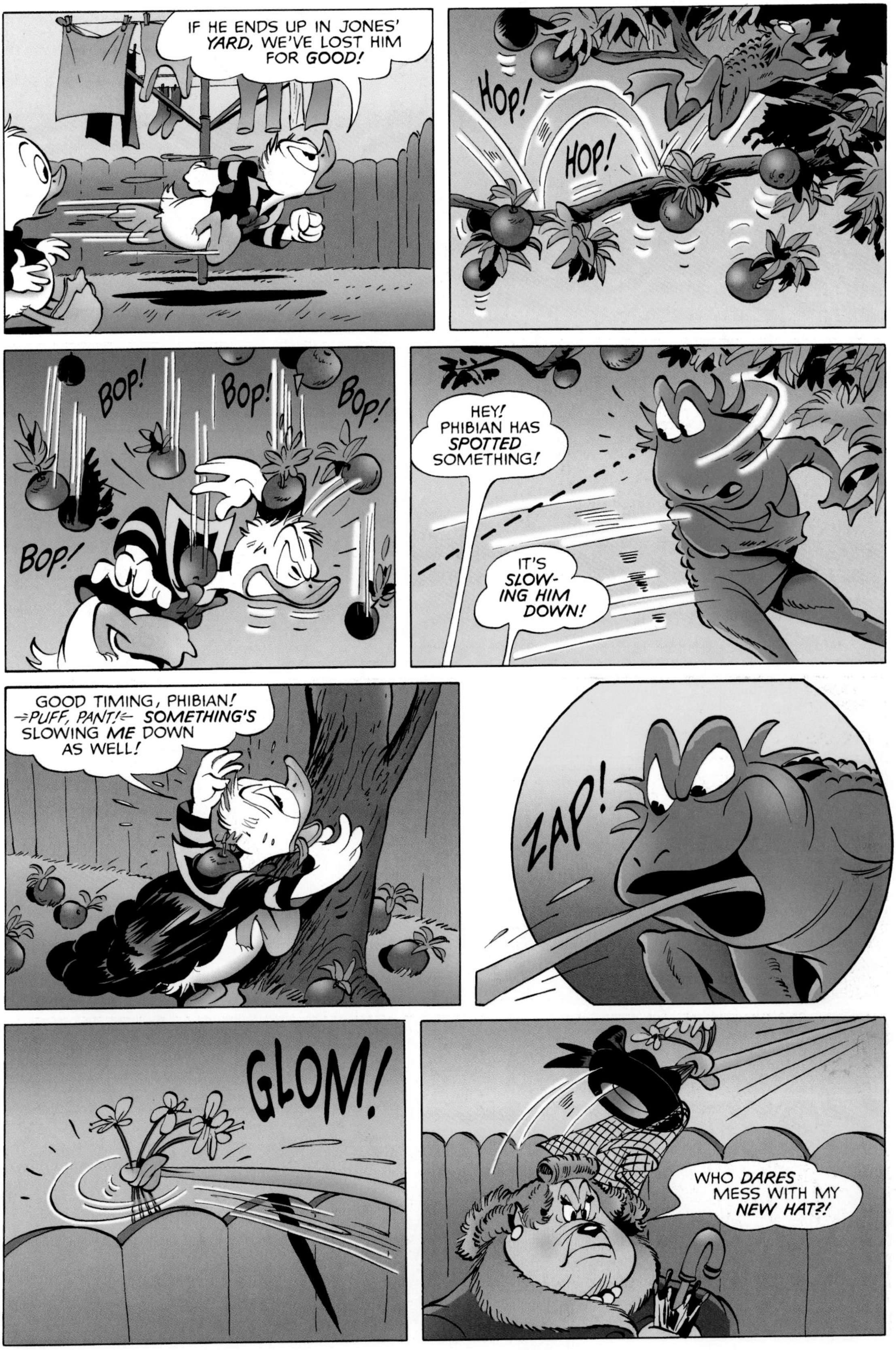
IF HE ENDS UP IN JONES' YARD, WE'VE LOST HIM FOR GOOD!
HOP!
HOP!
BOP!
BOP!
BOP!
BOP!
HEY! PHIBIAN HAS SPOTTED SOMETHING!
IT'S SLOWING HIM DOWN!
GOOD TIMING, PHIBIAN! -PUFF, PANT!- SOMETHING'S SLOWING ME DOWN AS WELL!
ZAP!
GLOM!
WHO DARES MESS WITH MY NEW HAT?!

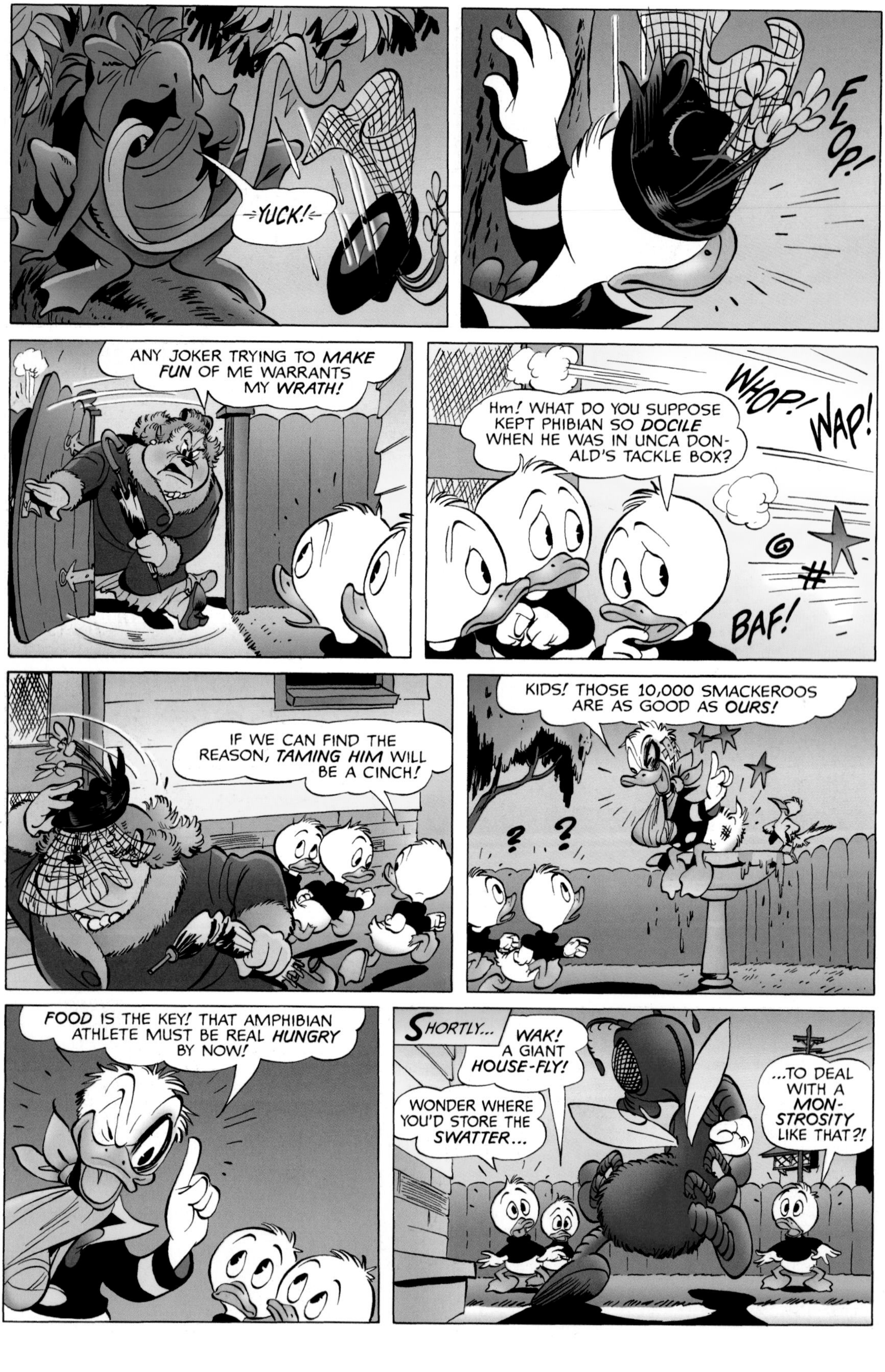
YUCK!
FLOP!
ANY JOKER TRYING TO MAKE FUN OF ME WARRANTS MY WRATH!
Hm! WHAT DO YOU SUPPOSE KEPT PHIBIAN SO DOCILE WHEN HE WAS IN UNCA DON-ALD'S TACKLE BOX?
WHOP! WAP!
BAF!
IF WE CAN FIND THE REASON, TAMING HIM WILL BE A CINCH!
KIDS! THOSE 10,000 SMACKEROOS ARE AS GOOD AS OURS!
FOOD IS THE KEY! THAT AMPHIBIAN ATHLETE MUST BE REAL HUNGRY BY NOW!
SHORTLY...
WAK! A GIANT HOUSE-FLY!
WONDER WHERE YOU'D STORE THE SWATTER...
...TO DEAL WITH A MON-STROSITY LIKE THAT?!

I REMEMBERED THIS *CARNIVAL SUIT* IN THE ATTIC! IT MUST MAKE ME LOOK *SUCCULENT* ENOUGH FOR PHIBIAN TO START CHASING *ME!*

HE'LL BE ABLE TO *SEE* ME BETTER IF I CLIMB UP *HIGHER!*

CLIK!

ROTATION-RELEASE LEVER

CROAK!

PHIBIAN'S LOCKED IN ON YOU *ALREADY,* UNCA DONALD!

ZIT!

ZOT!

YANK!

BULLS-EYE!

HEY!!! WHOO-AAAAAAAAA!!!

R-RIIP!

NOT VERY *TASTY,* Huh?

STOP THIS MERRY-GO-ROUND!!

=UGH!=

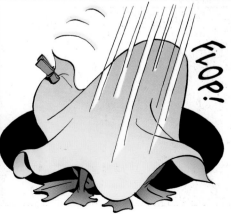

FLOP!

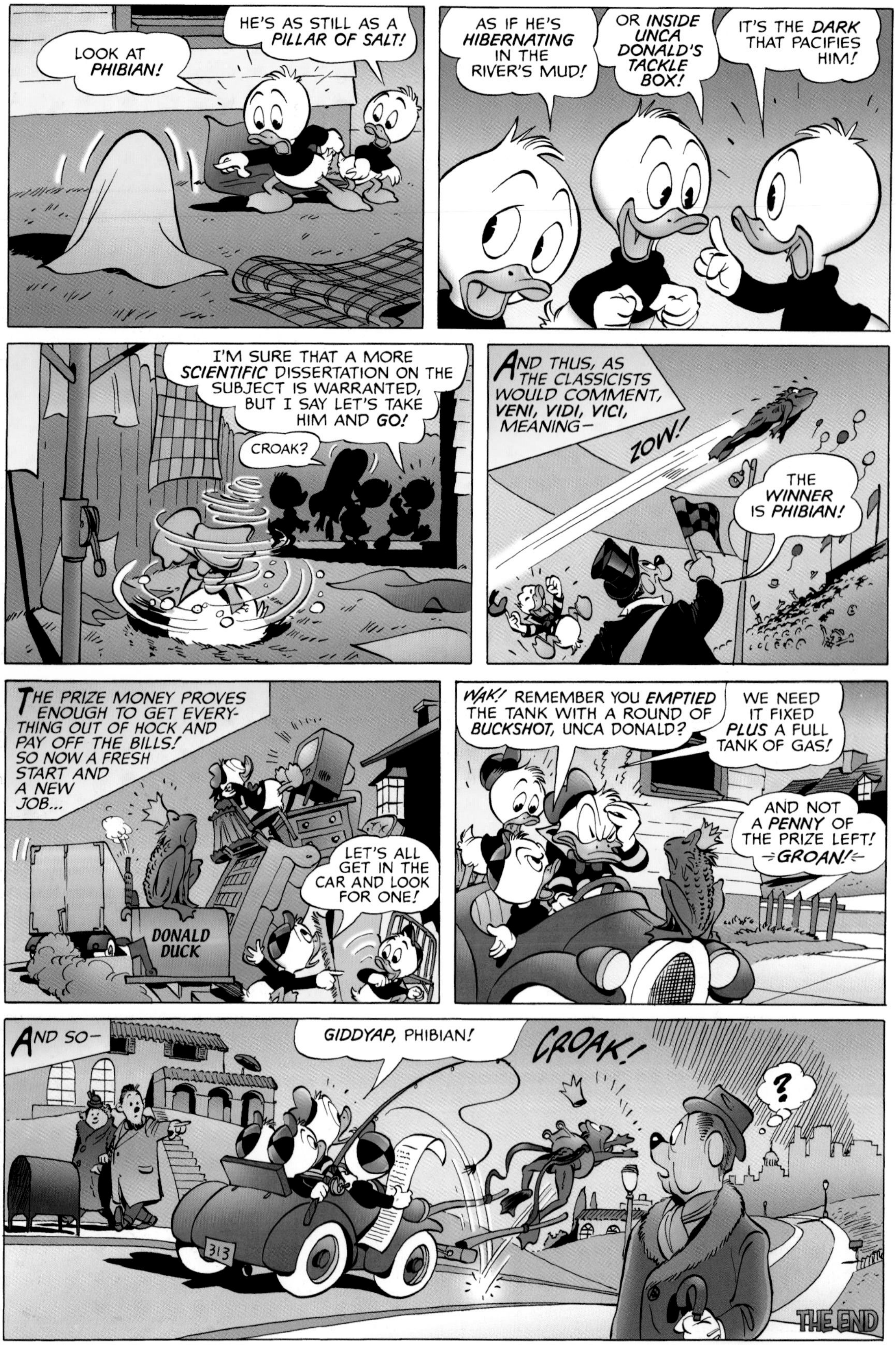
LOOK AT PHIBIAN!
HE'S AS STILL AS A PILLAR OF SALT!
AS IF HE'S HIBERNATING IN THE RIVER'S MUD!
OR INSIDE UNCA DONALD'S TACKLE BOX!
IT'S THE DARK THAT PACIFIES HIM!
I'M SURE THAT A MORE SCIENTIFIC DISSERTATION ON THE SUBJECT IS WARRANTED, BUT I SAY LET'S TAKE HIM AND GO!
CROAK?
AND THUS, AS THE CLASSICISTS WOULD COMMENT, VENI, VIDI, VICI, MEANING—
ZOW!
THE WINNER IS PHIBIAN!
THE PRIZE MONEY PROVES ENOUGH TO GET EVERYTHING OUT OF HOCK AND PAY OFF THE BILLS! SO NOW A FRESH START AND A NEW JOB...
LET'S ALL GET IN THE CAR AND LOOK FOR ONE!
DONALD DUCK
WAK! REMEMBER YOU EMPTIED THE TANK WITH A ROUND OF BUCKSHOT, UNCA DONALD?
WE NEED IT FIXED PLUS A FULL TANK OF GAS!
AND NOT A PENNY OF THE PRIZE LEFT! GROAN!
AND SO—
GIDDYAP, PHIBIAN!
CROAK!
?
313
THE END

Walt Disney's

Mickey Mouse in The Mystery of Freefer Hall

Part 1

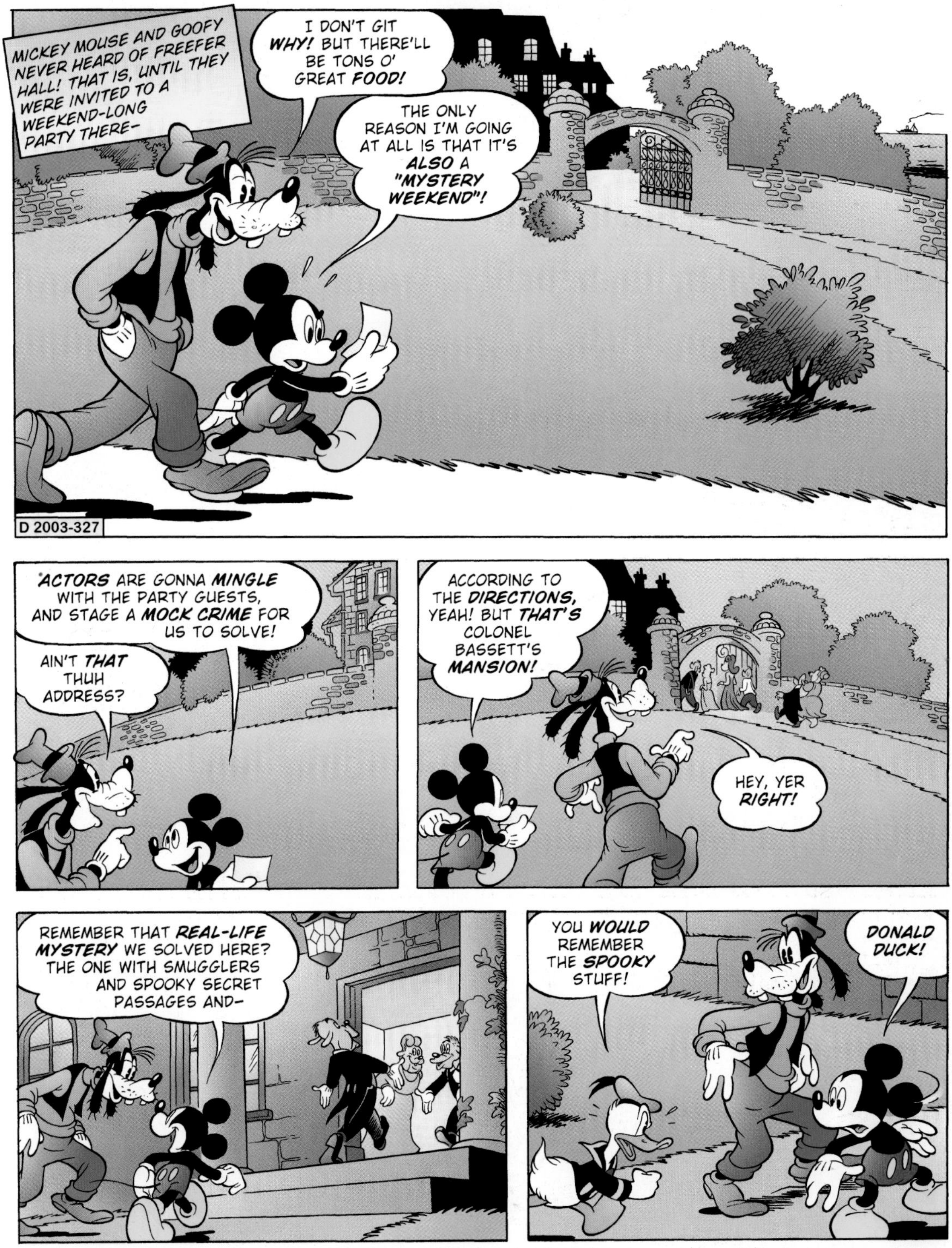

MICKEY MOUSE AND GOOFY NEVER HEARD OF FREEFER HALL! THAT IS, UNTIL THEY WERE INVITED TO A WEEKEND-LONG PARTY THERE–
I DON'T GIT WHY! BUT THERE'LL BE TONS O' GREAT FOOD!
THE ONLY REASON I'M GOING AT ALL IS THAT IT'S ALSO A "MYSTERY WEEKEND"!
D 2003-327
ACTORS ARE GONNA MINGLE WITH THE PARTY GUESTS, AND STAGE A MOCK CRIME FOR US TO SOLVE!
AIN'T THAT THUH ADDRESS?
ACCORDING TO THE DIRECTIONS, YEAH! BUT THAT'S COLONEL BASSETT'S MANSION!
HEY, YER RIGHT!
REMEMBER THAT REAL-LIFE MYSTERY WE SOLVED HERE? THE ONE WITH SMUGGLERS AND SPOOKY SECRET PASSAGES AND–
YOU WOULD REMEMBER THE SPOOKY STUFF!
DONALD DUCK!

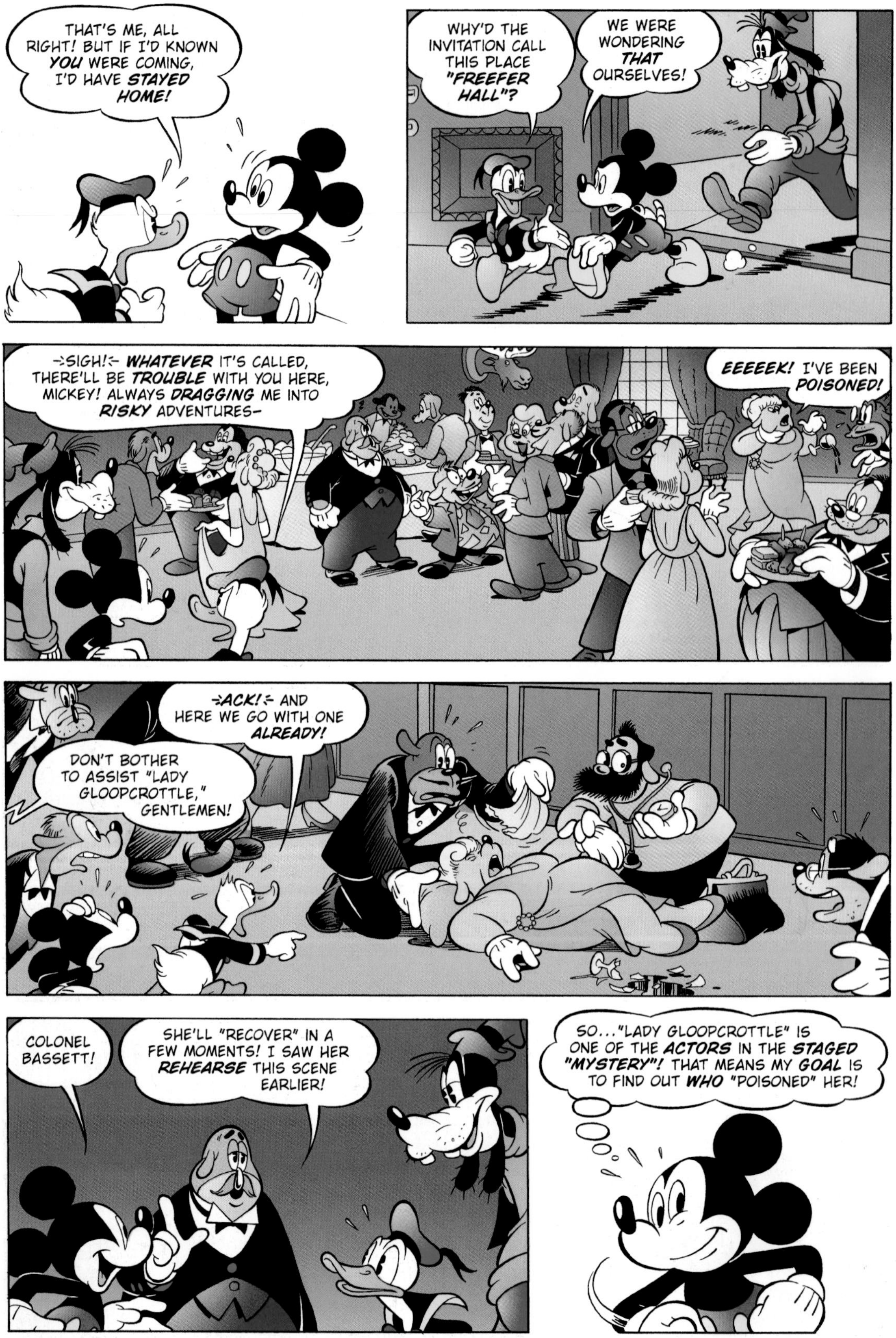
THAT'S ME, ALL RIGHT! BUT IF I'D KNOWN YOU WERE COMING, I'D HAVE STAYED HOME!
WHY'D THE INVITATION CALL THIS PLACE "FREEFER HALL"?
WE WERE WONDERING THAT OURSELVES!
-SIGH!- WHATEVER IT'S CALLED, THERE'LL BE TROUBLE WITH YOU HERE, MICKEY! ALWAYS DRAGGING ME INTO RISKY ADVENTURES—
EEEEEK! I'VE BEEN POISONED!
-ACK!- AND HERE WE GO WITH ONE ALREADY!
DON'T BOTHER TO ASSIST "LADY GLOOPCROTTLE," GENTLEMEN!
COLONEL BASSETT!
SHE'LL "RECOVER" IN A FEW MOMENTS! I SAW HER REHEARSE THIS SCENE EARLIER!
SO..."LADY GLOOPCROTTLE" IS ONE OF THE ACTORS IN THE STAGED "MYSTERY"! THAT MEANS MY GOAL IS TO FIND OUT WHO "POISONED" HER!

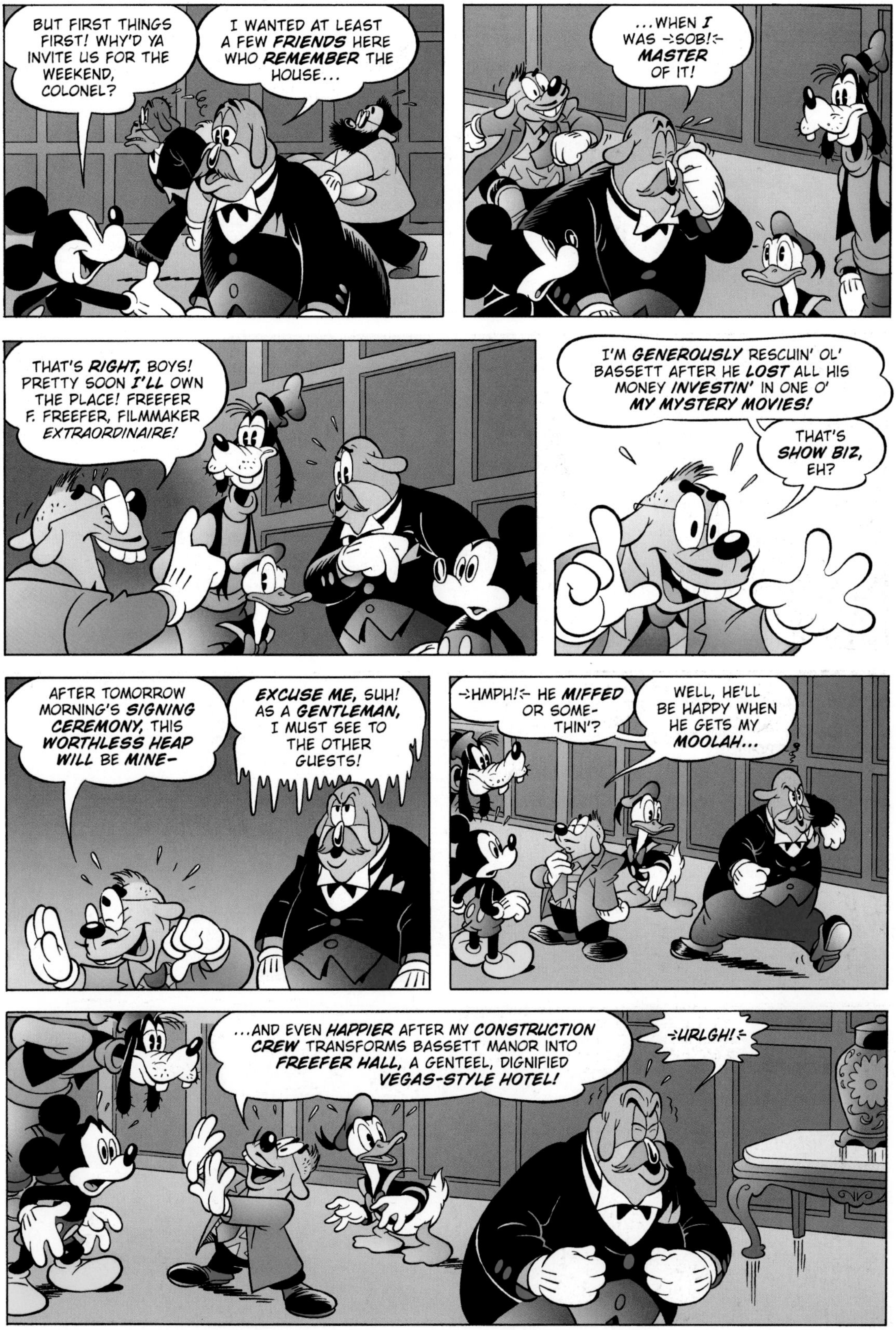
BUT FIRST THINGS FIRST! WHY'D YA INVITE US FOR THE WEEKEND, COLONEL?
I WANTED AT LEAST A FEW FRIENDS HERE WHO REMEMBER THE HOUSE...
...WHEN I WAS -SOB!- MASTER OF IT!
THAT'S RIGHT, BOYS! PRETTY SOON I'LL OWN THE PLACE! FREEFER F. FREEFER, FILMMAKER EXTRAORDINAIRE!
I'M GENEROUSLY RESCUIN' OL' BASSETT AFTER HE LOST ALL HIS MONEY INVESTIN' IN ONE O' MY MYSTERY MOVIES!
THAT'S SHOW BIZ, EH?
AFTER TOMORROW MORNING'S SIGNING CEREMONY, THIS WORTHLESS HEAP WILL BE MINE-
EXCUSE ME, SUH! AS A GENTLEMAN, I MUST SEE TO THE OTHER GUESTS!
-HMPH!- HE MIFFED OR SOME-THIN'?
WELL, HE'LL BE HAPPY WHEN HE GETS MY MOOLAH...
...AND EVEN HAPPIER AFTER MY CONSTRUCTION CREW TRANSFORMS BASSETT MANOR INTO FREEFER HALL, A GENTEEL, DIGNIFIED VEGAS-STYLE HOTEL!
-URLGH!-

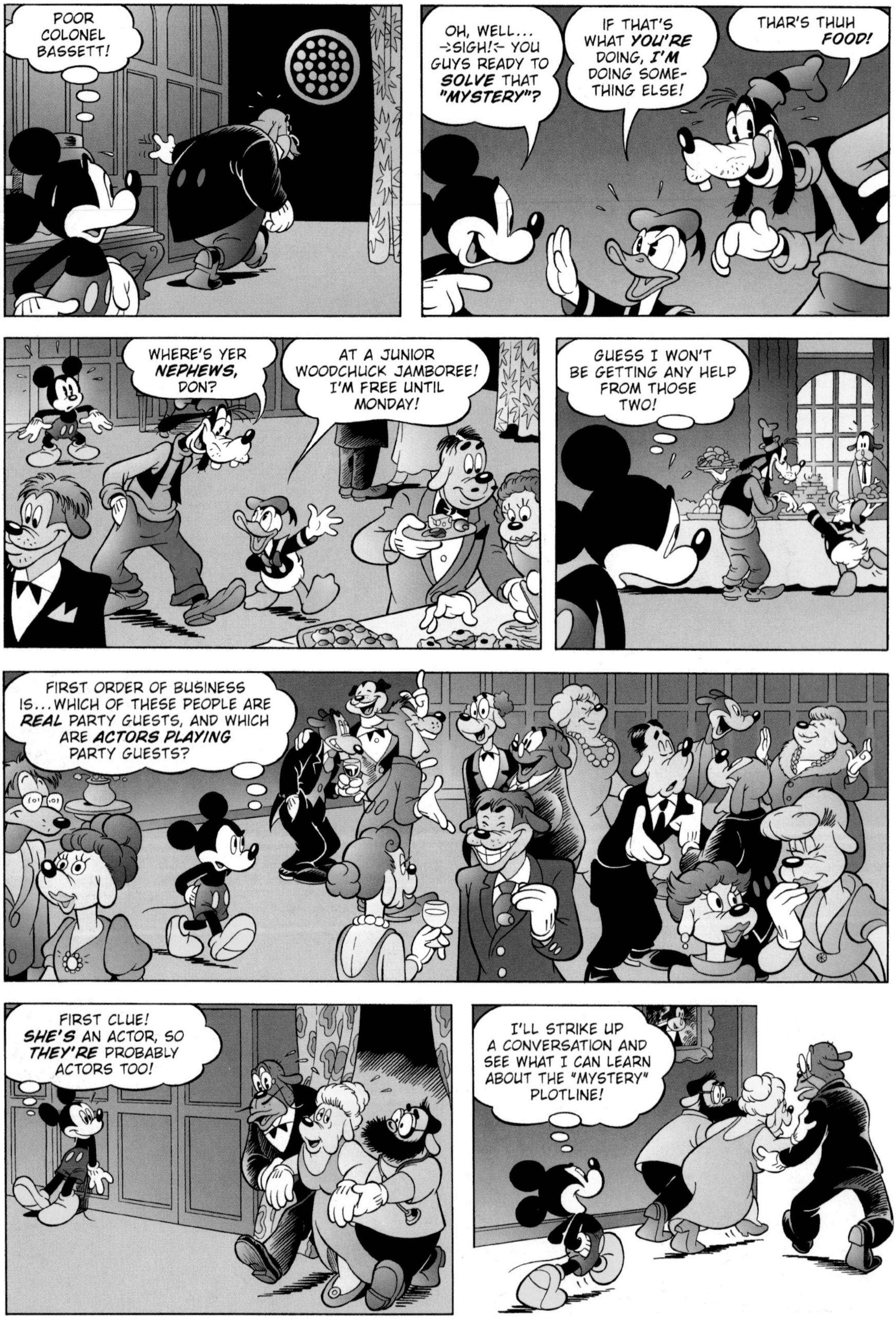
POOR COLONEL BASSETT!
OH, WELL... ⇢SIGH!⇠ YOU GUYS READY TO SOLVE THAT "MYSTERY"?
IF THAT'S WHAT YOU'RE DOING, I'M DOING SOMETHING ELSE!
THAR'S THUH FOOD!
WHERE'S YER NEPHEWS, DON?
AT A JUNIOR WOODCHUCK JAMBOREE! I'M FREE UNTIL MONDAY!
GUESS I WON'T BE GETTING ANY HELP FROM THOSE TWO!
FIRST ORDER OF BUSINESS IS...WHICH OF THESE PEOPLE ARE REAL PARTY GUESTS, AND WHICH ARE ACTORS PLAYING PARTY GUESTS?
FIRST CLUE! SHE'S AN ACTOR, SO THEY'RE PROBABLY ACTORS TOO!
I'LL STRIKE UP A CONVERSATION AND SEE WHAT I CAN LEARN ABOUT THE "MYSTERY" PLOTLINE!

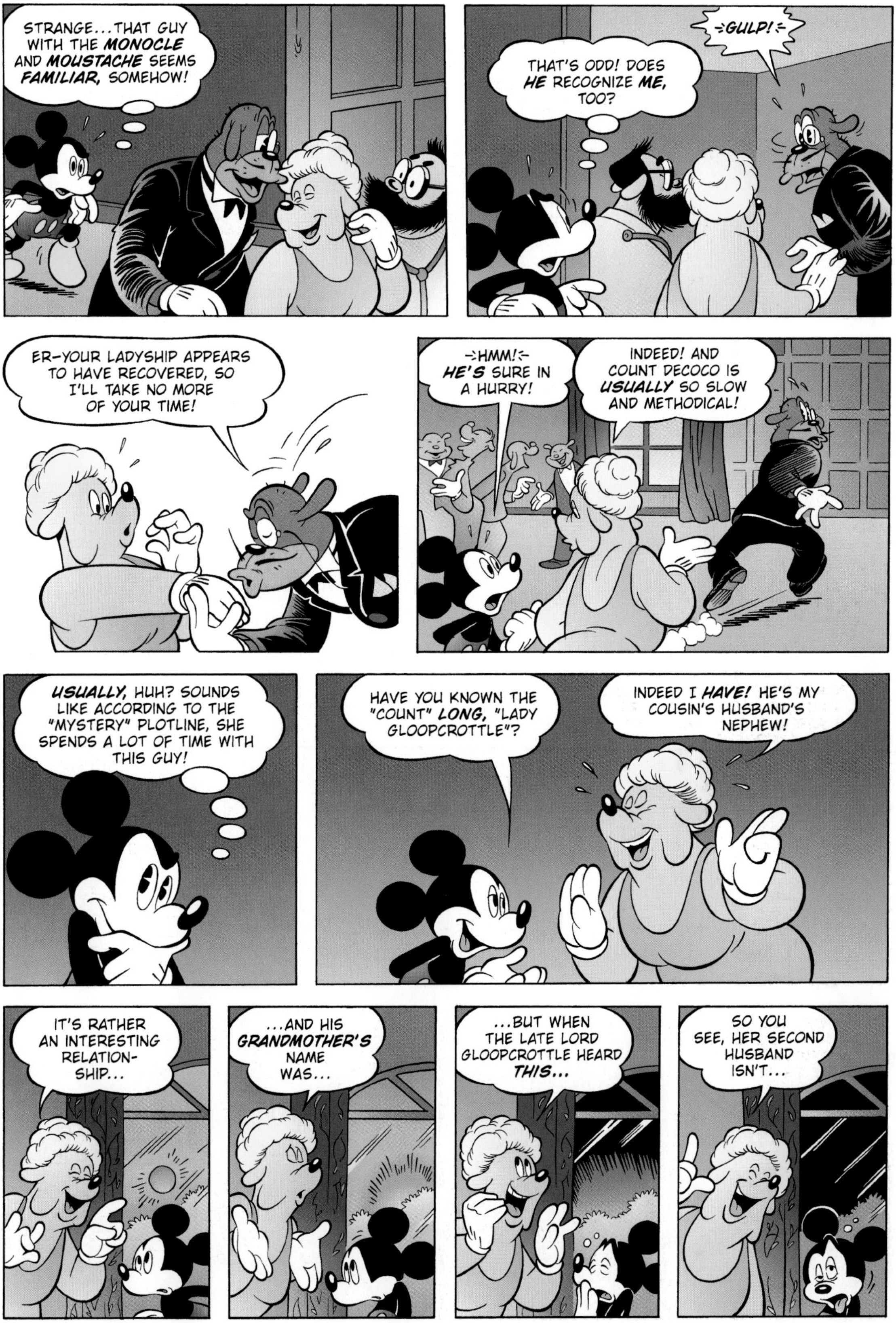
STRANGE...THAT GUY WITH THE MONOCLE AND MOUSTACHE SEEMS FAMILIAR, SOMEHOW!
GULP!
THAT'S ODD! DOES HE RECOGNIZE ME, TOO?
ER—YOUR LADYSHIP APPEARS TO HAVE RECOVERED, SO I'LL TAKE NO MORE OF YOUR TIME!
HMM! HE'S SURE IN A HURRY!
INDEED! AND COUNT DECOCO IS USUALLY SO SLOW AND METHODICAL!
USUALLY, HUH? SOUNDS LIKE ACCORDING TO THE "MYSTERY" PLOTLINE, SHE SPENDS A LOT OF TIME WITH THIS GUY!
HAVE YOU KNOWN THE "COUNT" LONG, "LADY GLOOPCROTTLE"?
INDEED I HAVE! HE'S MY COUSIN'S HUSBAND'S NEPHEW!
IT'S RATHER AN INTERESTING RELATION-SHIP...
...AND HIS GRANDMOTHER'S NAME WAS...
...BUT WHEN THE LATE LORD GLOOPCROTTLE HEARD THIS...
SO YOU SEE, HER SECOND HUSBAND ISN'T...

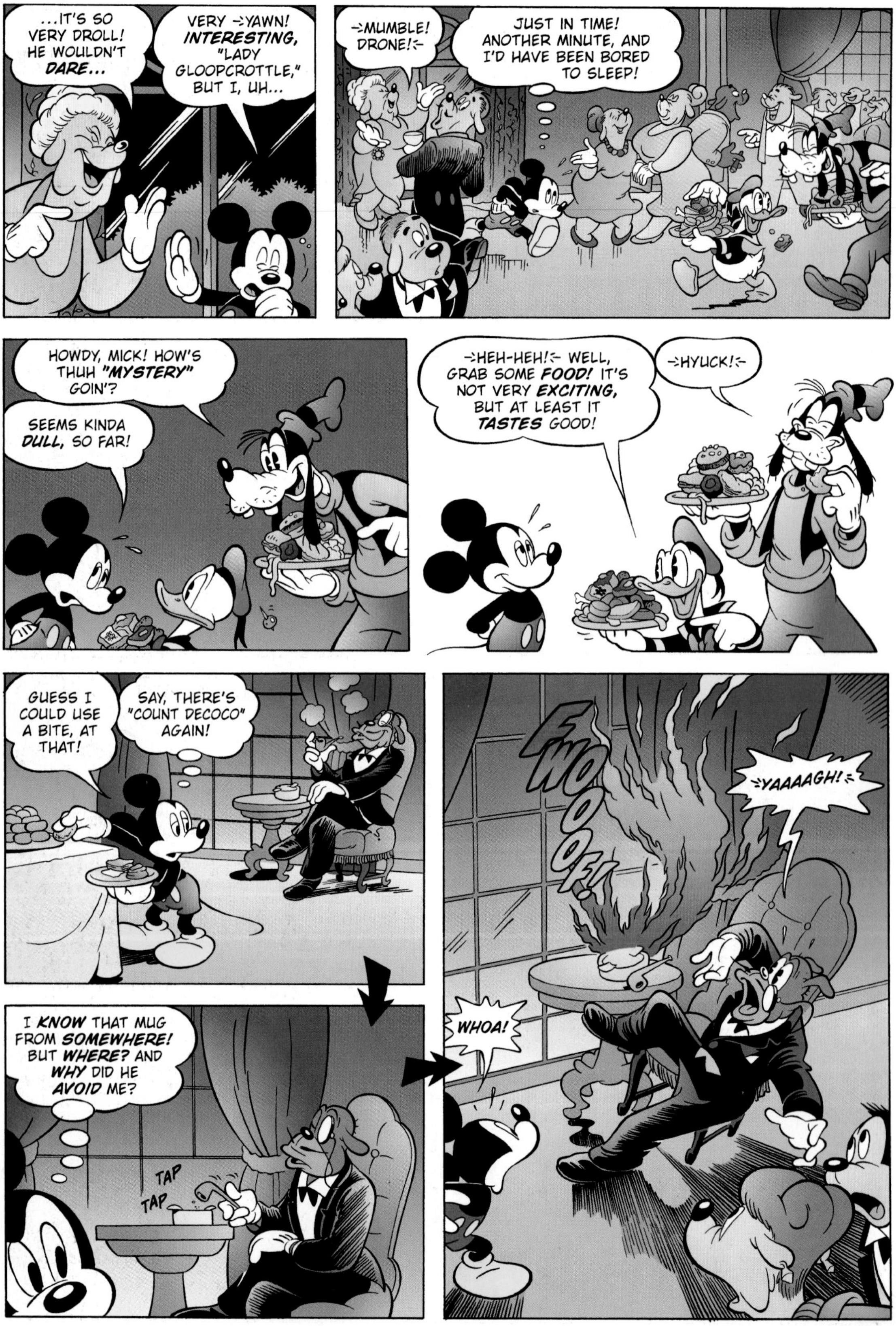
...IT'S SO VERY DROLL! HE WOULDN'T DARE...
VERY ~YAWN! INTERESTING, "LADY GLOOPCROTTLE," BUT I, UH...
~MUMBLE! DRONE!~
JUST IN TIME! ANOTHER MINUTE, AND I'D HAVE BEEN BORED TO SLEEP!
HOWDY, MICK! HOW'S THUH "MYSTERY" GOIN'?
SEEMS KINDA DULL, SO FAR!
~HEH-HEH!~ WELL, GRAB SOME FOOD! IT'S NOT VERY EXCITING, BUT AT LEAST IT TASTES GOOD!
~HYUCK!~
GUESS I COULD USE A BITE, AT THAT!
SAY, THERE'S "COUNT DECOCO" AGAIN!
I KNOW THAT MUG FROM SOMEWHERE! BUT WHERE? AND WHY DID HE AVOID ME?
TAP
TAP
FWOOOOF!!
~YAAAAGH!~
WHOA!

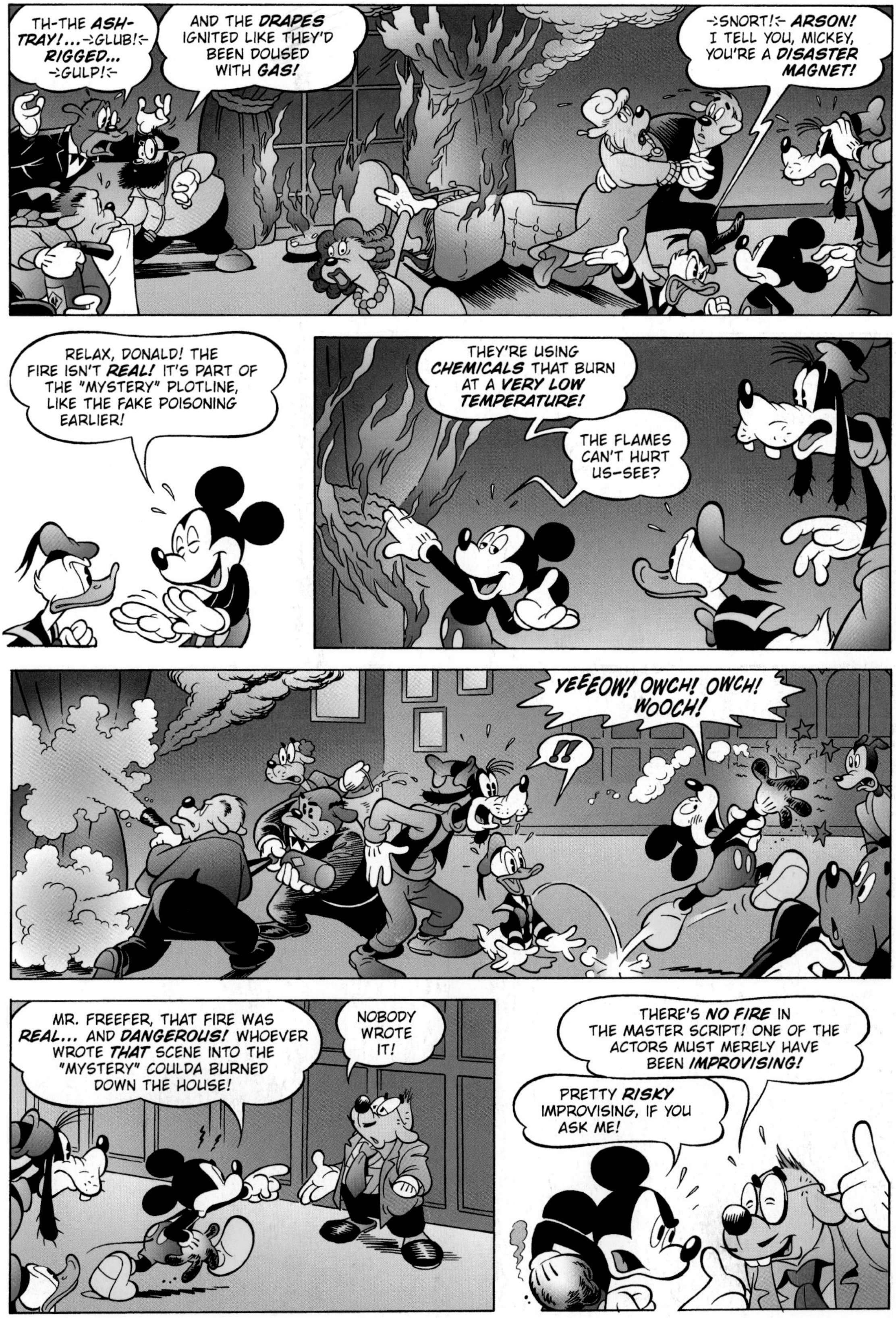
TH-THE ASH-TRAY!... ->GLUB!<- RIGGED... ->GULP!<-
AND THE DRAPES IGNITED LIKE THEY'D BEEN DOUSED WITH GAS!
->SNORT!<- ARSON! I TELL YOU, MICKEY, YOU'RE A DISASTER MAGNET!
RELAX, DONALD! THE FIRE ISN'T REAL! IT'S PART OF THE "MYSTERY" PLOTLINE, LIKE THE FAKE POISONING EARLIER!
THEY'RE USING CHEMICALS THAT BURN AT A VERY LOW TEMPERATURE!
THE FLAMES CAN'T HURT US—SEE?
YEEEOW! OWCH! OWCH! WOOCH!
!!
MR. FREEFER, THAT FIRE WAS REAL... AND DANGEROUS! WHOEVER WROTE THAT SCENE INTO THE "MYSTERY" COULDA BURNED DOWN THE HOUSE!
NOBODY WROTE IT!
THERE'S NO FIRE IN THE MASTER SCRIPT! ONE OF THE ACTORS MUST MERELY HAVE BEEN IMPROVISING!
PRETTY RISKY IMPROVISING, IF YOU ASK ME!

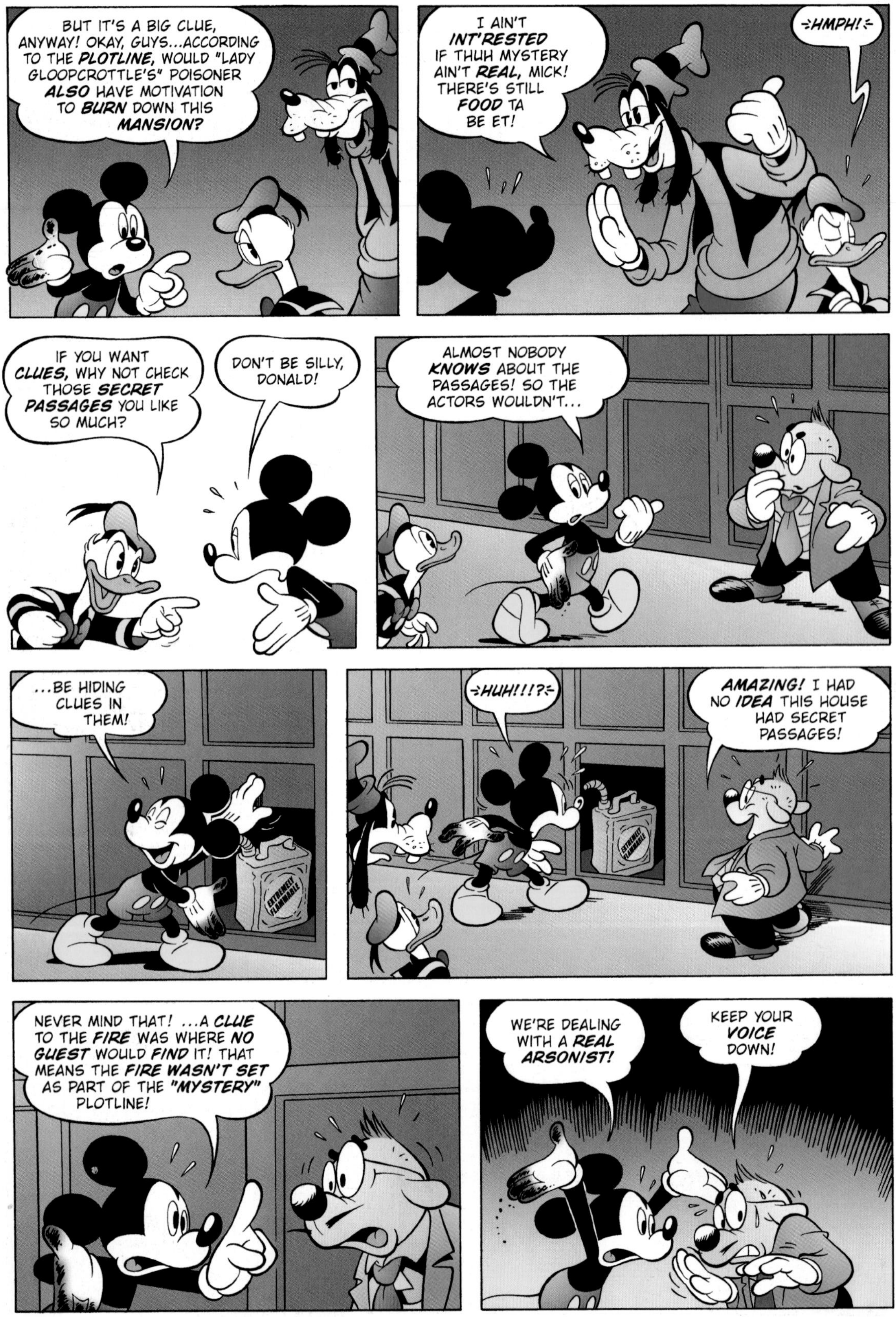
BUT IT'S A BIG CLUE, ANYWAY! OKAY, GUYS...ACCORDING TO THE PLOTLINE, WOULD "LADY GLOOPCROTTLE'S" POISONER ALSO HAVE MOTIVATION TO BURN DOWN THIS MANSION?
I AIN'T INT'RESTED IF THUH MYSTERY AIN'T REAL, MICK! THERE'S STILL FOOD TA BE ET!
HMPH!
IF YOU WANT CLUES, WHY NOT CHECK THOSE SECRET PASSAGES YOU LIKE SO MUCH?
DON'T BE SILLY, DONALD!
ALMOST NOBODY KNOWS ABOUT THE PASSAGES! SO THE ACTORS WOULDN'T...
...BE HIDING CLUES IN THEM!
EXTREMELY FLAMMABLE
HUH!!!?
EXTREMELY FLAMMABLE
AMAZING! I HAD NO IDEA THIS HOUSE HAD SECRET PASSAGES!
NEVER MIND THAT! ...A CLUE TO THE FIRE WAS WHERE NO GUEST WOULD FIND IT! THAT MEANS THE FIRE WASN'T SET AS PART OF THE "MYSTERY" PLOTLINE!
WE'RE DEALING WITH A REAL ARSONIST!
KEEP YOUR VOICE DOWN!

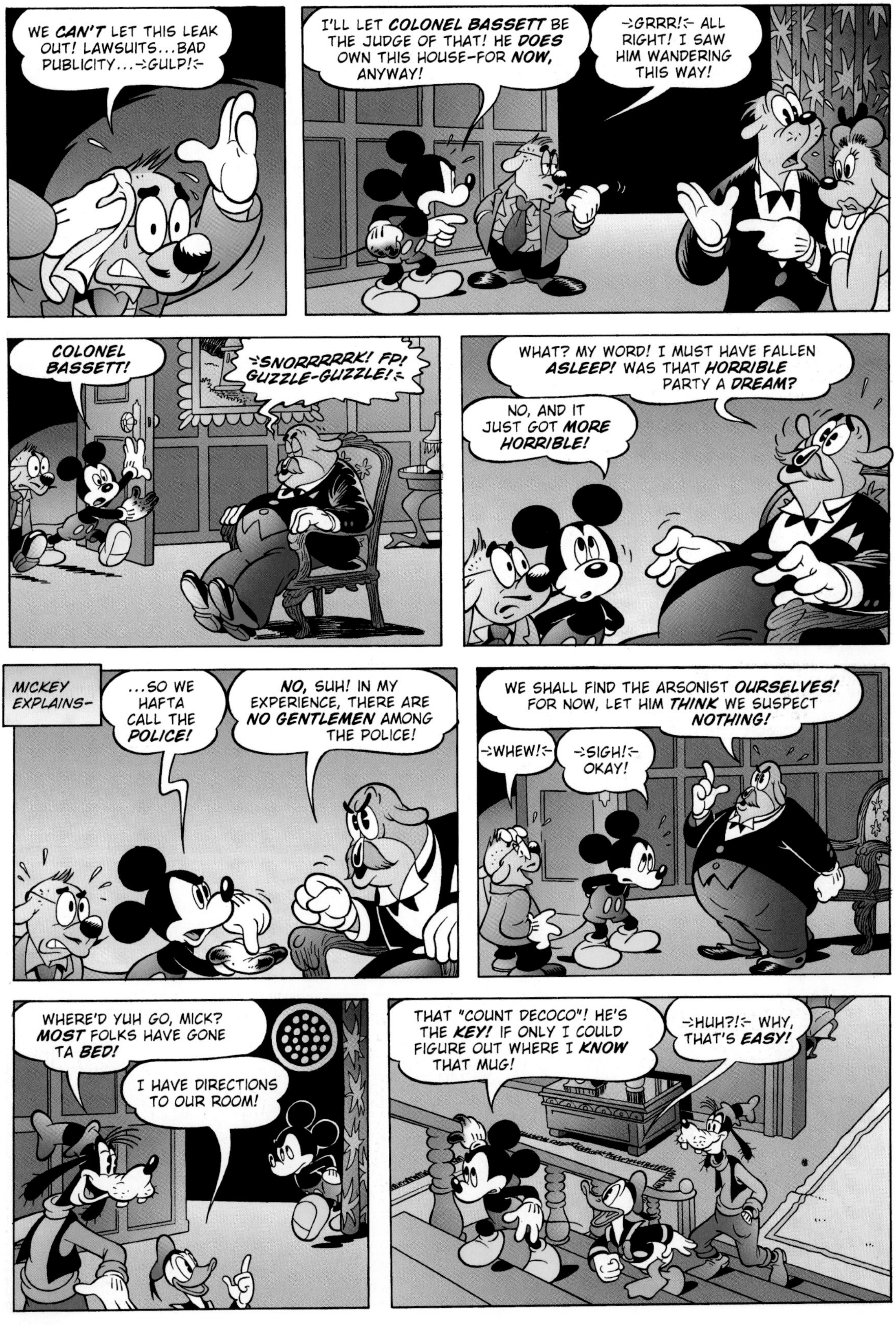
WE CAN'T LET THIS LEAK OUT! LAWSUITS...BAD PUBLICITY...⇒GULP!⇐
I'LL LET COLONEL BASSETT BE THE JUDGE OF THAT! HE DOES OWN THIS HOUSE—FOR NOW, ANYWAY!
⇒GRRR!⇐ ALL RIGHT! I SAW HIM WANDERING THIS WAY!
COLONEL BASSETT!
⇒SNORRRRRK! FP! GUZZLE-GUZZLE!⇐
WHAT? MY WORD! I MUST HAVE FALLEN ASLEEP! WAS THAT HORRIBLE PARTY A DREAM?
NO, AND IT JUST GOT MORE HORRIBLE!
MICKEY EXPLAINS—
...SO WE HAFTA CALL THE POLICE!
NO, SUH! IN MY EXPERIENCE, THERE ARE NO GENTLEMEN AMONG THE POLICE!
WE SHALL FIND THE ARSONIST OURSELVES! FOR NOW, LET HIM THINK WE SUSPECT NOTHING!
⇒WHEW!⇐
⇒SIGH!⇐ OKAY!
WHERE'D YUH GO, MICK? MOST FOLKS HAVE GONE TA BED!
I HAVE DIRECTIONS TO OUR ROOM!
THAT "COUNT DECOCO"! HE'S THE KEY! IF ONLY I COULD FIGURE OUT WHERE I KNOW THAT MUG!
⇒HUH?!⇐ WHY, THAT'S EASY!

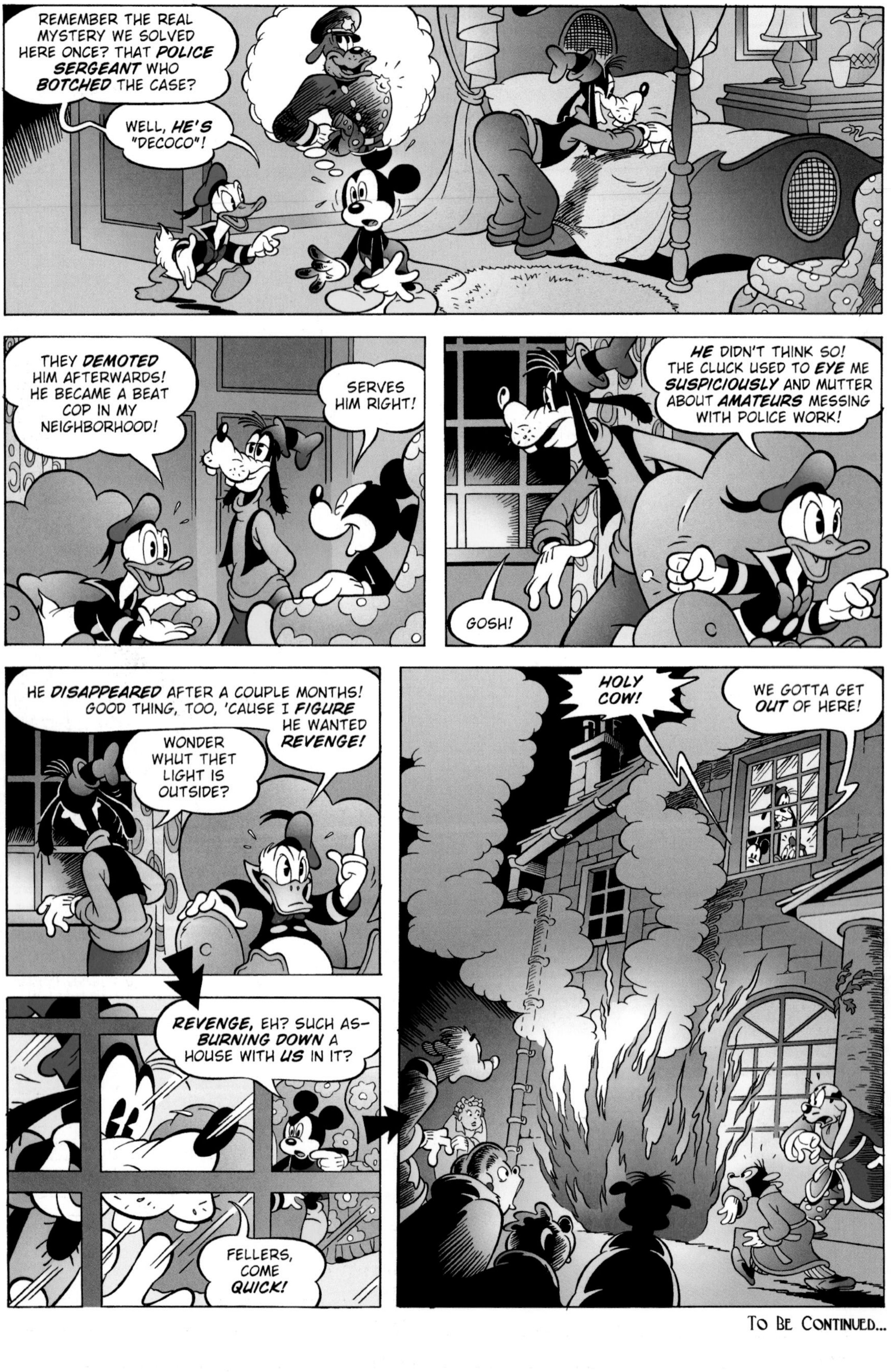
REMEMBER THE REAL MYSTERY WE SOLVED HERE ONCE? THAT POLICE SERGEANT WHO BOTCHED THE CASE?
WELL, HE'S "DECOCO"!
THEY DEMOTED HIM AFTERWARDS! HE BECAME A BEAT COP IN MY NEIGHBORHOOD!
SERVES HIM RIGHT!
HE DIDN'T THINK SO! THE CLUCK USED TO EYE ME SUSPICIOUSLY AND MUTTER ABOUT AMATEURS MESSING WITH POLICE WORK!
GOSH!
HE DISAPPEARED AFTER A COUPLE MONTHS! GOOD THING, TOO, 'CAUSE I FIGURE HE WANTED REVENGE!
WONDER WHUT THET LIGHT IS OUTSIDE?
REVENGE, EH? SUCH AS BURNING DOWN A HOUSE WITH US IN IT?
FELLERS, COME QUICK!
HOLY COW!
WE GOTTA GET OUT OF HERE!

TO BE CONTINUED...

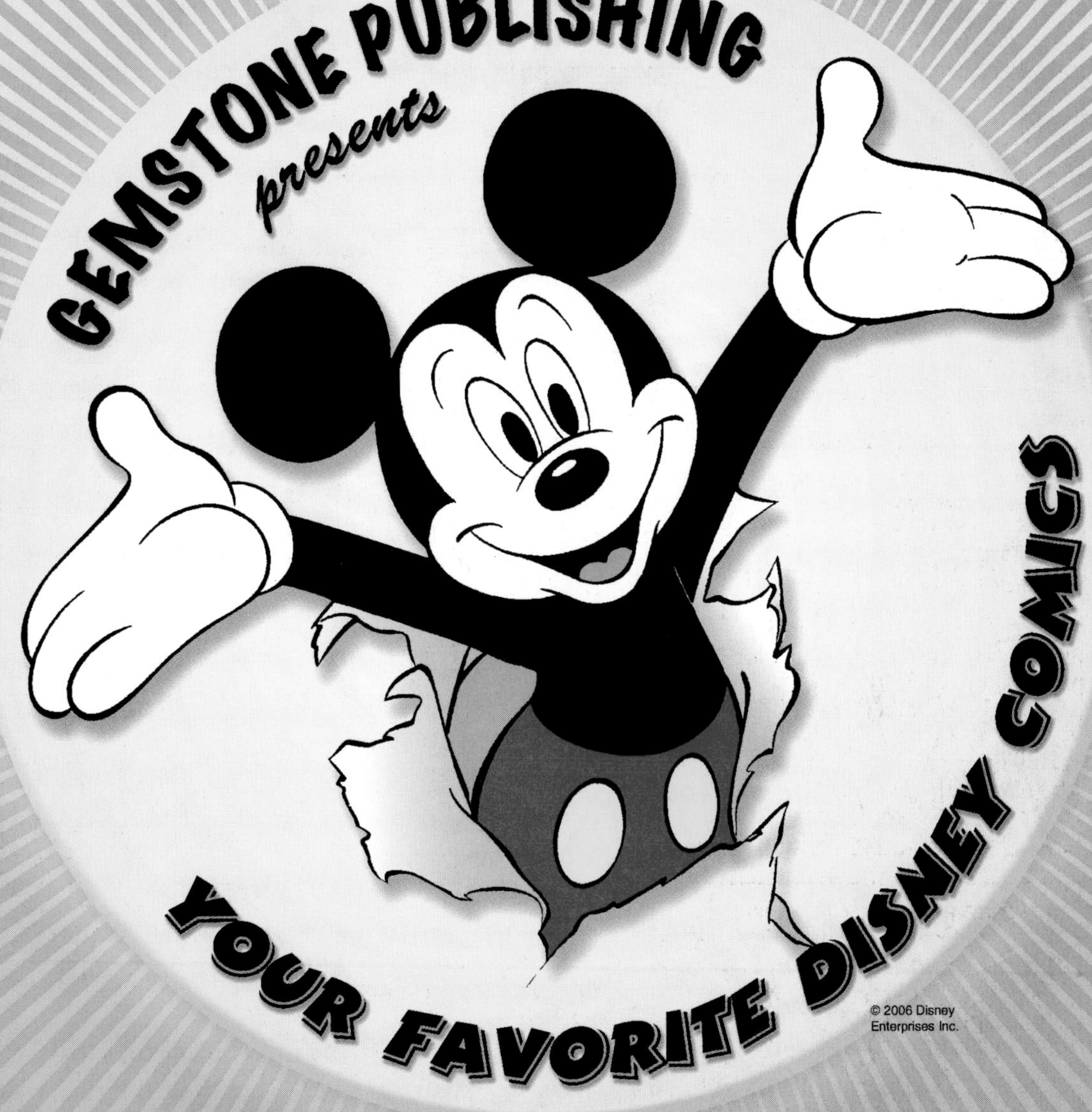

GEMSTONE PUBLISHING
presents
YOUR FAVORITE DISNEY COMICS

Delivered right to your door!

We know how much you enjoy visiting your local comic shop, but wouldn't it be nice to have your favorite Disney comics delivered to you? Subscribe today and we'll send the latest issues of your favorite comics directly to your doorstep. And if you would still prefer to browse through the latest in comic art but aren't sure where to go, check out the Comic Shop Locator Service at www.diamondcomics.com/csls or call 1-888-COMIC-BOOK.

MAIL THIS COUPON TO:

Gemstone Publishing • P.O. Box 469 • West Plains, Missouri 65775

- ☐ ***Walt Disney's Comics & Stories:*** $83.40 for 12 issues, 64 pages ($90.00 Canada, payable in US funds) .... $ ________
- ☐ ***Walt Disney's Donald Duck & Friends:*** $35.40 for 12 issues, 32 pages ($40.00 Canada, payable in US funds) .... $ ________
- ☐ ***Walt Disney's Uncle Scrooge:*** $83.40 for 12 issues, 64 pages ($90.00 Canada, payable in US funds) .... $ ________
- ☐ ***Walt Disney's Mickey Mouse & Friends:*** $35.40 for 12 issues, 32 pages ($40.00 Canada, payable in US funds) .... $ ________
- ☐ ***Donald Duck Adventures:*** $95.40 for 12 bimonthly issues, 128 pages ($105.00 Canada, payable in US funds) .... $ ________
- ☐ ***Mickey Mouse Adventures:*** $95.40 for 12 bimonthly issues, 128 pages ($105.00 Canada, payable in US funds) .... $ ________

SUBTOTAL: $ ________

SALES TAX (MO residents add 6.975% sales tax; MD residents add 5% sales tax): $ ________

TOTAL: $ ________

Name: ____________________

Address: ____________________

____

City: ________ State: ________ Zip: ________

Email: ____________________

CREDIT CARD:

☐ Visa

☐ MasterCard

☐ Other

Card #: ____________________

Exp. Date: ____________________

ULP!

ARE YOU A DONALDIST?

don • ald • ism \ dän'-ld-iz'-em \ *n* : the research of Disney comics, and/or the fan culture that is found among Disney comics aficionados (Jon Gisle, 1973)

Go on, admit it. You like reading about comics history... but you love reading historically important comics themselves. You want a real Disney comics archival book—a thick trade paperback full of those extra-esoteric Duck and Mouse tales that just wouldn't fit in anywhere else.

You're a Donaldist! And we know where you're coming from.

Dive into the 160-page
DISNEY COMICS: 75 YEARS OF INNOVATION *for:*

- *Great Donald sagas by Carl Barks (a newly-restored "Race to the South Seas"), Don Rosa ("Fortune on the Rocks"), and Al Taliaferro (the seminal "Donald's Nephews")*
- *Never-before-reprinted Mickey tales by Floyd Gottfredson ("Mickey Mouse Music") and Romano Scarpa ("AKA Cormorant Number Twelve")*
- *Ducks by Daan Jippes, Dick Kinney, William Van Horn, and Daniel Branca*
- *Mice by Byron Erickson, César Ferioli and Paul Murry*
- *Renato Canini's José Carioca, Gil Turner's Big Bad Wolf—and Brer Rabbit too!*

GEMSTONE PUBLISHING *presents*
WALT DISNEY TREASURES VOLUME ONE
Now On Sale

(Any similarity between this book and the Disney DVDs you love to collect is purely intentional!)

© 2006 Disney Enterprises, Inc.

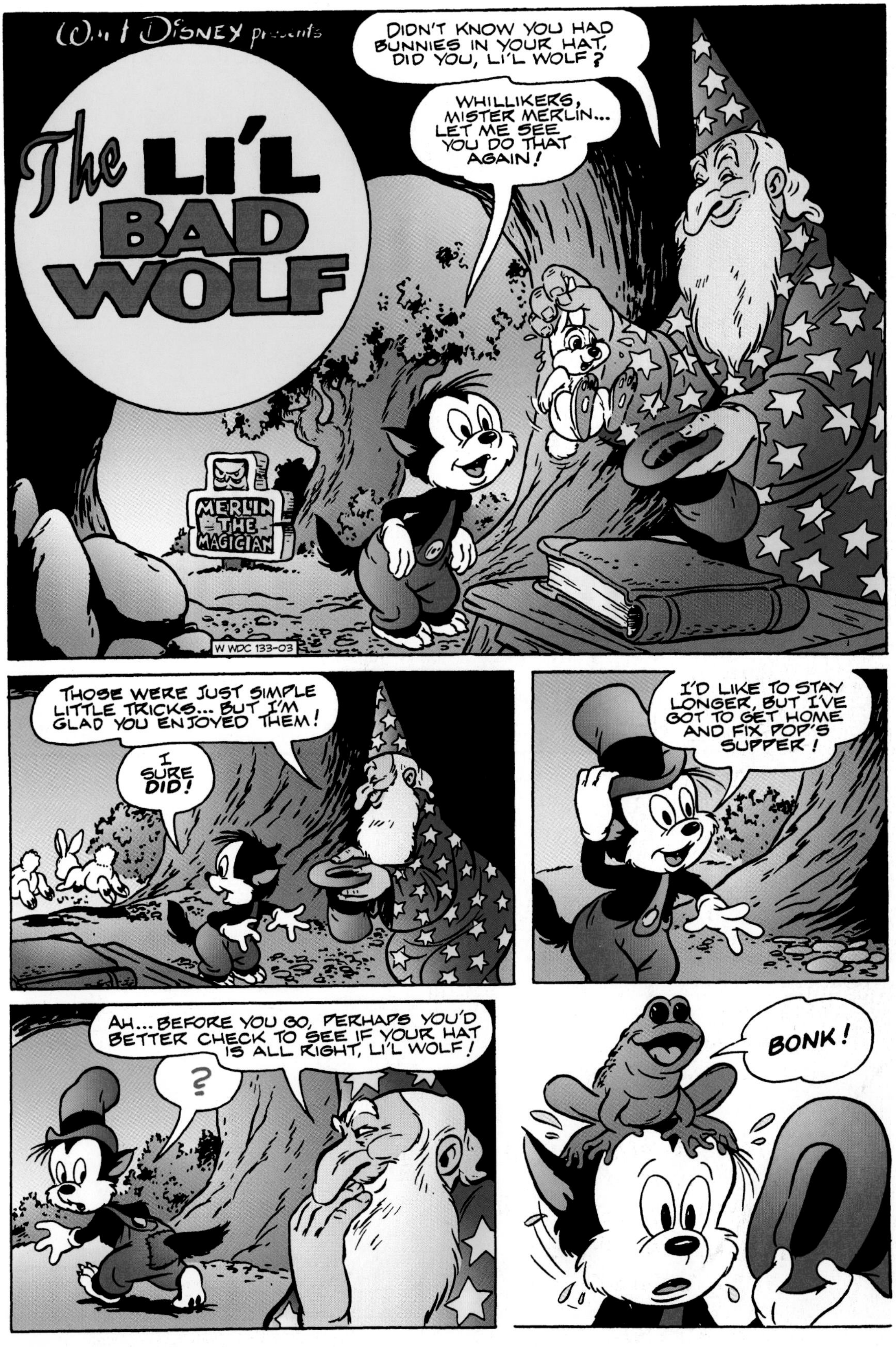
Walt Disney presents
The LI'L BAD WOLF
DIDN'T KNOW YOU HAD BUNNIES IN YOUR HAT, DID YOU, LI'L WOLF?
WHILLIKERS, MISTER MERLIN... LET ME SEE YOU DO THAT AGAIN!
MERLIN THE MAGICIAN
W WDC 133-03
THOSE WERE JUST SIMPLE LITTLE TRICKS... BUT I'M GLAD YOU ENJOYED THEM!
I SURE DID!
I'D LIKE TO STAY LONGER, BUT I'VE GOT TO GET HOME AND FIX POP'S SUPPER!
AH... BEFORE YOU GO, PERHAPS YOU'D BETTER CHECK TO SEE IF YOUR HAT IS ALL RIGHT, LI'L WOLF!
?
BONK!

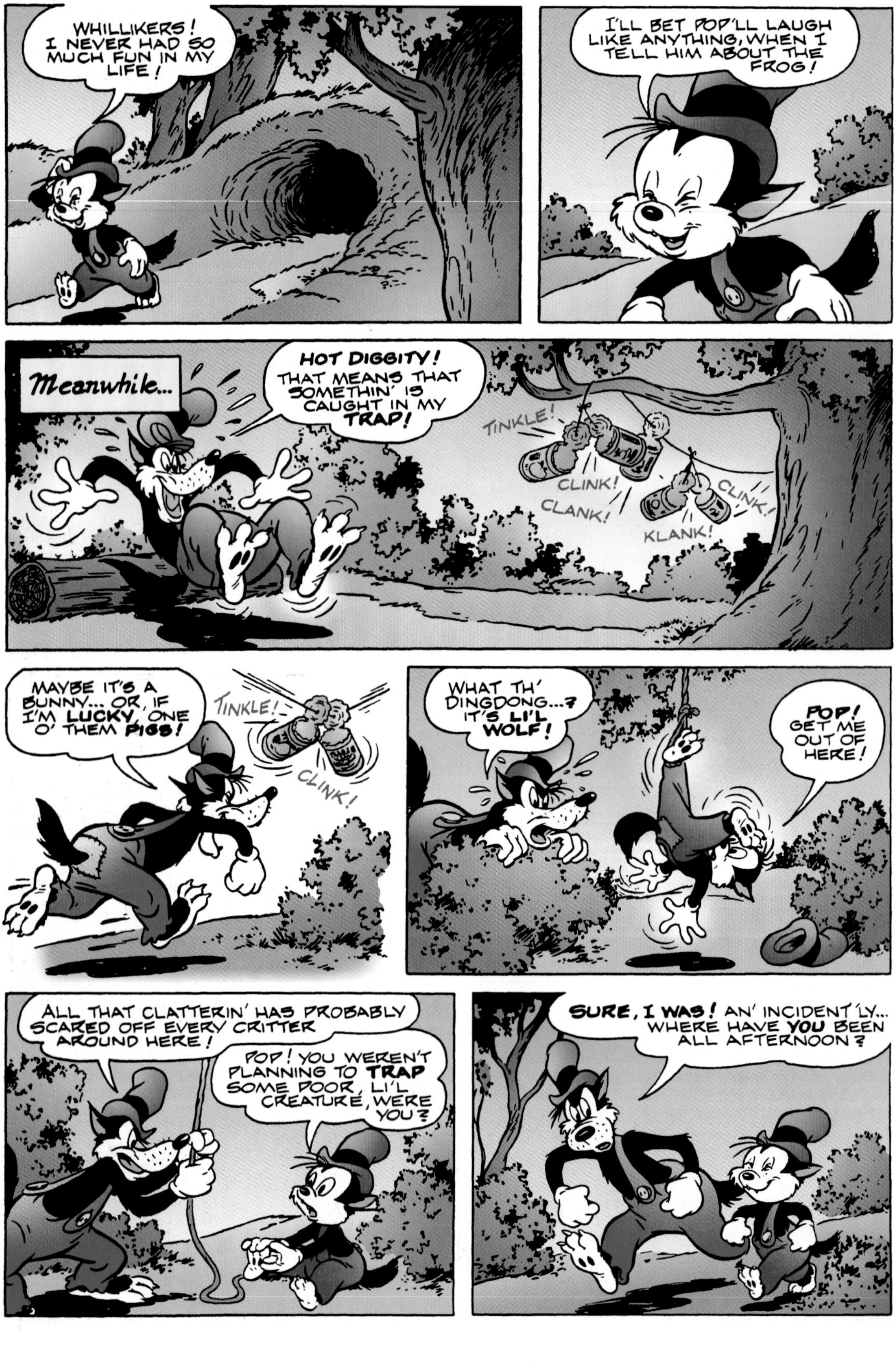
WHILLIKERS! I NEVER HAD SO MUCH FUN IN MY LIFE!
I'LL BET POP'LL LAUGH LIKE ANYTHING, WHEN I TELL HIM ABOUT THE FROG!
Meanwhile...
HOT DIGGITY! THAT MEANS THAT SOMETHIN' IS CAUGHT IN MY TRAP!
TINKLE!
CLINK!
CLANK!
CLINK!
KLANK!
MAYBE IT'S A BUNNY... OR, IF I'M LUCKY, ONE O' THEM PIGS!
TINKLE!
CLINK!
WHAT TH' DINGDONG...? IT'S LI'L WOLF!
POP! GET ME OUT OF HERE!
ALL THAT CLATTERIN' HAS PROBABLY SCARED OFF EVERY CRITTER AROUND HERE!
POP! YOU WEREN'T PLANNING TO TRAP SOME POOR, LI'L CREATURE, WERE YOU?
SURE, I WAS! AN' INCIDENT'LY... WHERE HAVE YOU BEEN ALL AFTERNOON?

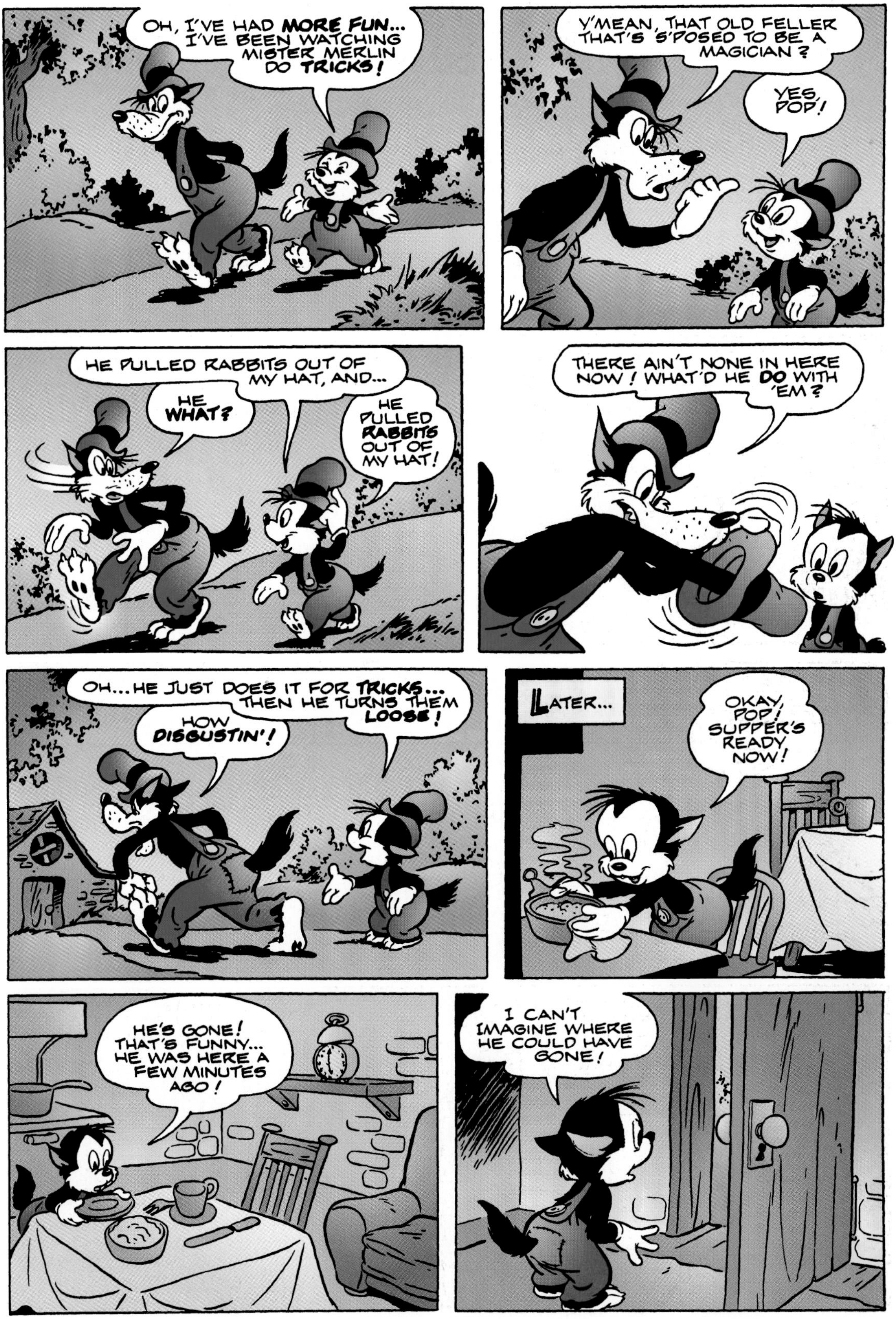
OH, I'VE HAD MORE FUN... I'VE BEEN WATCHING MISTER MERLIN DO TRICKS!
Y'MEAN, THAT OLD FELLER THAT'S S'POSED TO BE A MAGICIAN?
YES, POP!
HE PULLED RABBITS OUT OF MY HAT, AND...
HE WHAT?
HE PULLED RABBITS OUT OF MY HAT!
THERE AIN'T NONE IN HERE NOW! WHAT'D HE DO WITH 'EM?
OH... HE JUST DOES IT FOR TRICKS... THEN HE TURNS THEM LOOSE!
HOW DISGUSTIN'!
LATER...
OKAY, POP! SUPPER'S READY NOW!
HE'S GONE! THAT'S FUNNY... HE WAS HERE A FEW MINUTES AGO!
I CAN'T IMAGINE WHERE HE COULD HAVE GONE!

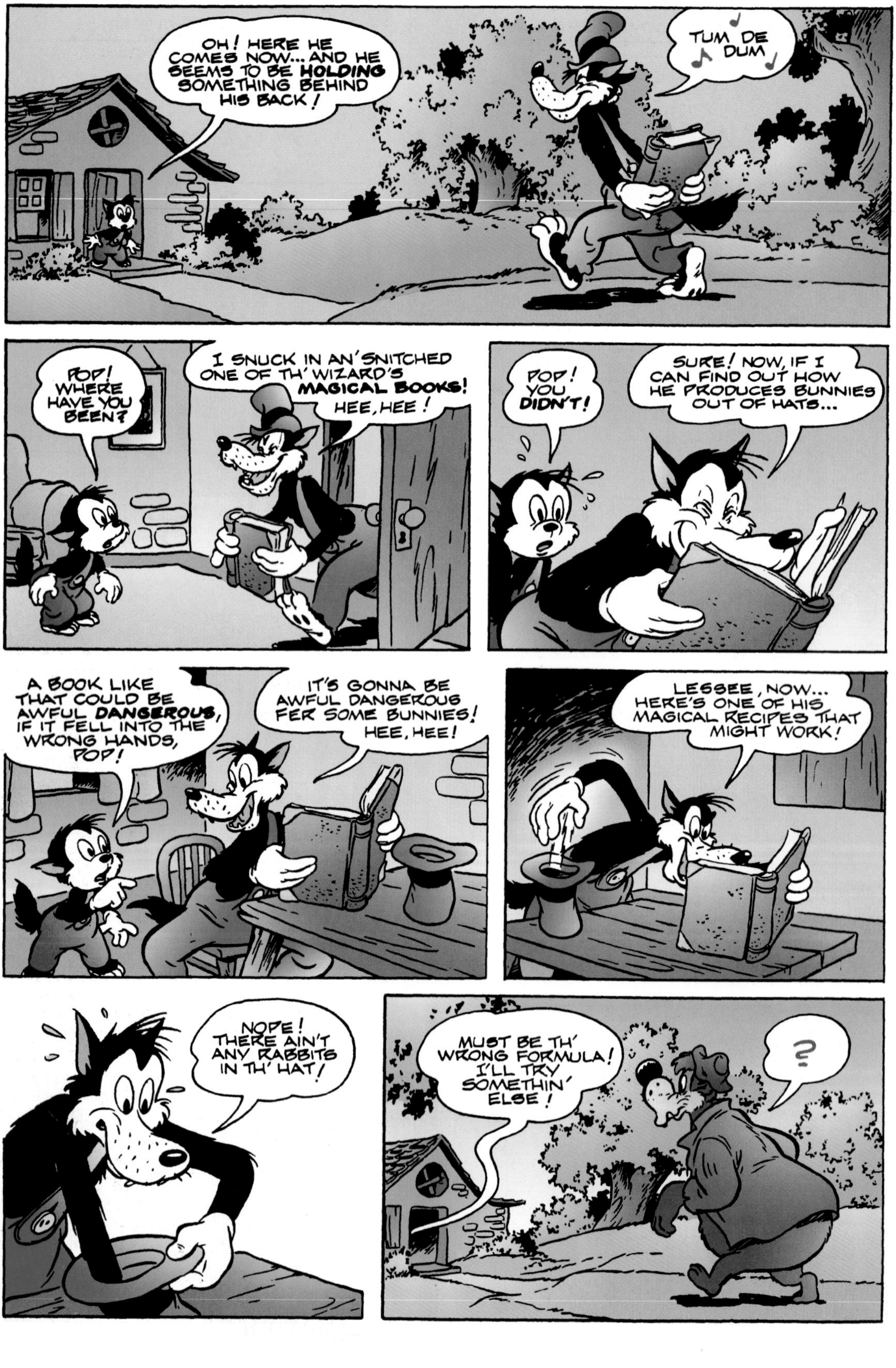
OH! HERE HE COMES NOW...AND HE SEEMS TO BE HOLDING SOMETHING BEHIND HIS BACK!
TUM DE DUM
POP! WHERE HAVE YOU BEEN?
I SNUCK IN AN' SNITCHED ONE OF TH' WIZARD'S MAGICAL BOOKS! HEE, HEE!
POP! YOU DIDN'T!
SURE! NOW, IF I CAN FIND OUT HOW HE PRODUCES BUNNIES OUT OF HATS...
A BOOK LIKE THAT COULD BE AWFUL DANGEROUS, IF IT FELL INTO THE WRONG HANDS, POP!
IT'S GONNA BE AWFUL DANGEROUS FER SOME BUNNIES! HEE, HEE!
LESSEE, NOW... HERE'S ONE OF HIS MAGICAL RECIPES THAT MIGHT WORK!
NOPE! THERE AIN'T ANY RABBITS IN TH' HAT!
MUST BE TH' WRONG FORMULA! I'LL TRY SOMETHIN' ELSE!
?

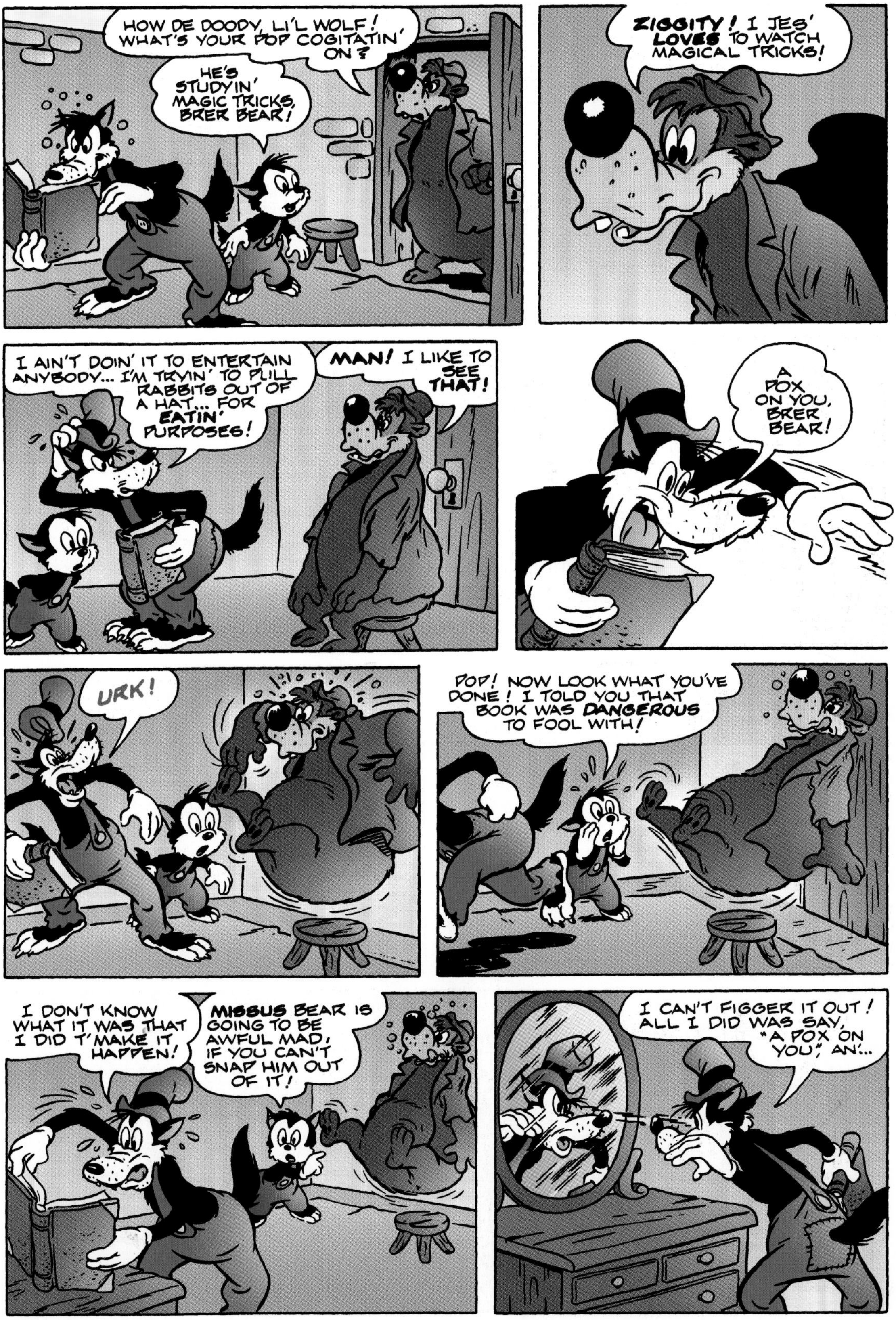
HOW DE DOODY, LI'L WOLF! WHAT'S YOUR POP COGITATIN' ON?
HE'S STUDYIN' MAGIC TRICKS, BRER BEAR!
ZIGGITY! I JES' LOVES TO WATCH MAGICAL TRICKS!
I AIN'T DOIN' IT TO ENTERTAIN ANYBODY... I'M TRYIN' TO PULL RABBITS OUT OF A HAT... FOR EATIN' PURPOSES!
MAN! I LIKE TO SEE THAT!
A POX ON YOU, BRER BEAR!
URK!
POP! NOW LOOK WHAT YOU'VE DONE! I TOLD YOU THAT BOOK WAS DANGEROUS TO FOOL WITH!
I DON'T KNOW WHAT IT WAS THAT I DID T'MAKE IT HAPPEN!
MISSUS BEAR IS GOING TO BE AWFUL MAD, IF YOU CAN'T SNAP HIM OUT OF IT!
I CAN'T FIGGER IT OUT! ALL I DID WAS SAY, "A POX ON YOU," AN'...

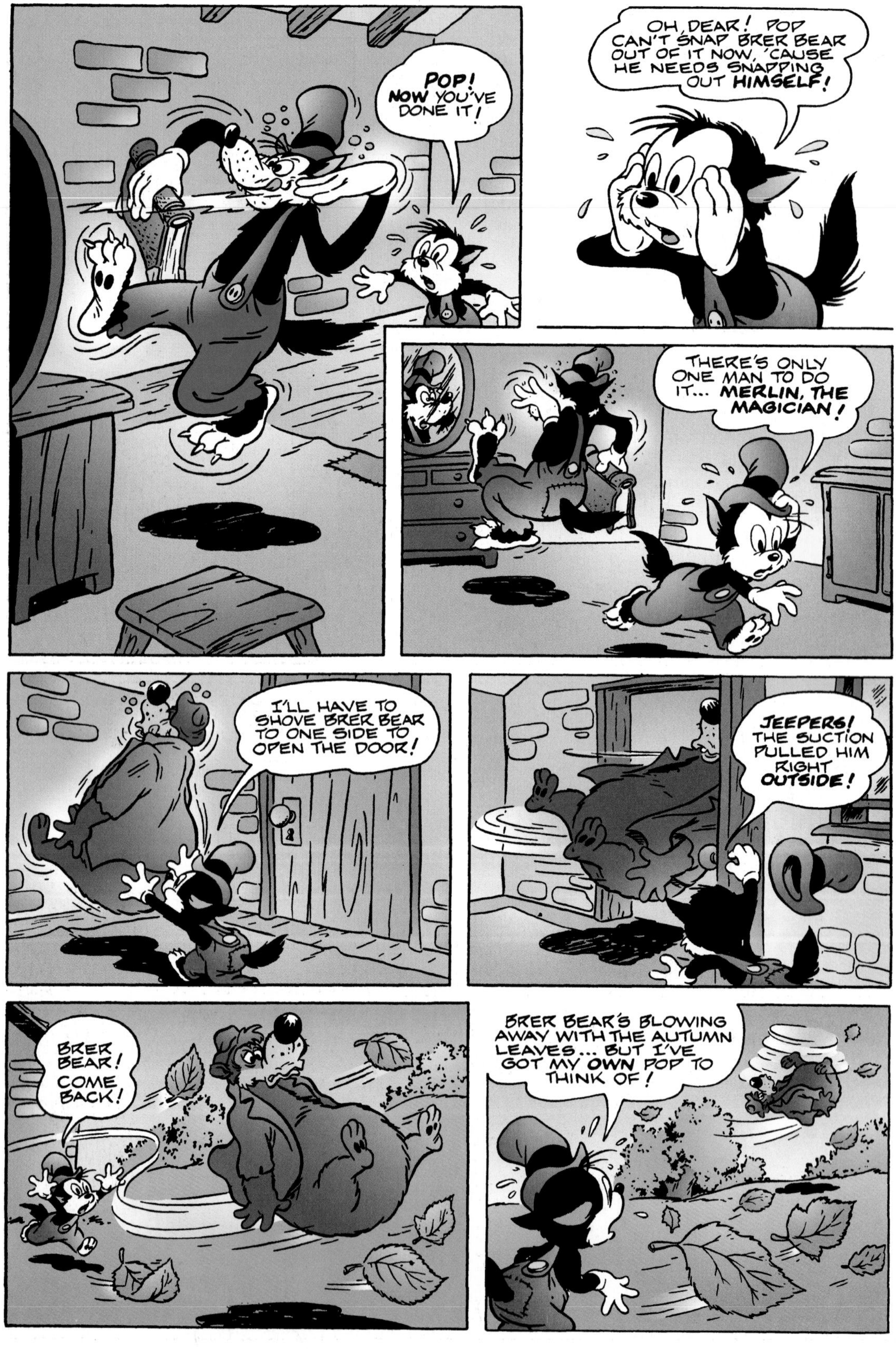
POP! NOW YOU'VE DONE IT!
OH, DEAR! POP CAN'T SNAP BRER BEAR OUT OF IT NOW, 'CAUSE HE NEEDS SNAPPING OUT HIMSELF!
THERE'S ONLY ONE MAN TO DO IT... MERLIN, THE MAGICIAN!
I'LL HAVE TO SHOVE BRER BEAR TO ONE SIDE TO OPEN THE DOOR!
JEEPERS! THE SUCTION PULLED HIM RIGHT OUTSIDE!
BRER BEAR! COME BACK!
BRER BEAR'S BLOWING AWAY WITH THE AUTUMN LEAVES... BUT I'VE GOT MY OWN POP TO THINK OF!

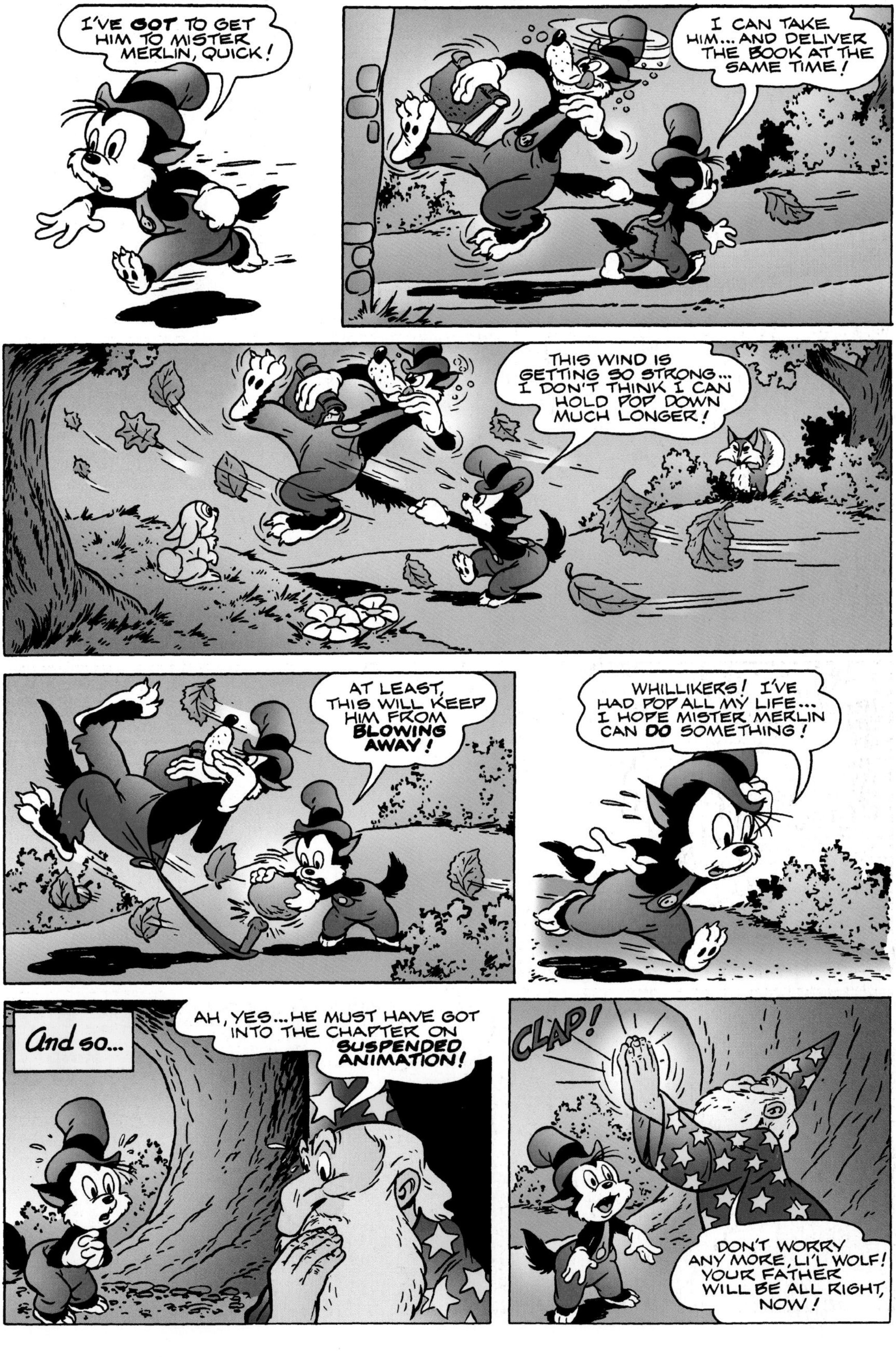
I'VE GOT TO GET HIM TO MISTER MERLIN, QUICK!
I CAN TAKE HIM... AND DELIVER THE BOOK AT THE SAME TIME!
THIS WIND IS GETTING SO STRONG... I DON'T THINK I CAN HOLD POP DOWN MUCH LONGER!
AT LEAST, THIS WILL KEEP HIM FROM BLOWING AWAY!
WHILLIKERS! I'VE HAD POP ALL MY LIFE... I HOPE MISTER MERLIN CAN DO SOMETHING!
And so...
AH, YES... HE MUST HAVE GOT INTO THE CHAPTER ON SUSPENDED ANIMATION!
CLAP!
DON'T WORRY ANY MORE, LI'L WOLF! YOUR FATHER WILL BE ALL RIGHT, NOW!

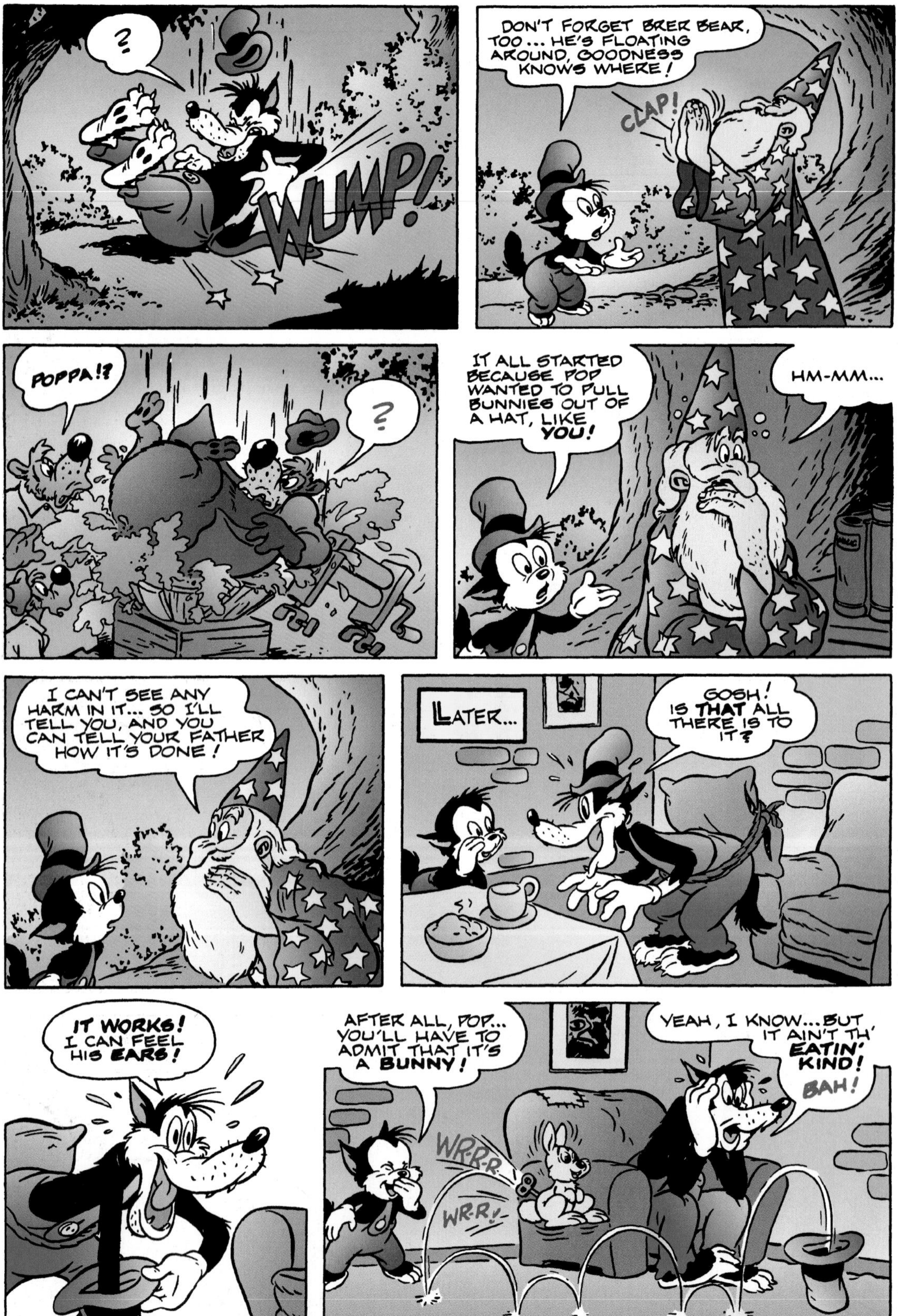
?
WUMP!
DON'T FORGET BRER BEAR, TOO... HE'S FLOATING AROUND, GOODNESS KNOWS WHERE!
CLAP!
POPPA!?
?
IT ALL STARTED BECAUSE POP WANTED TO PULL BUNNIES OUT OF A HAT, LIKE YOU!
HM-MM...
I CAN'T SEE ANY HARM IN IT... SO I'LL TELL YOU, AND YOU CAN TELL YOUR FATHER HOW IT'S DONE!
LATER...
GOSH! IS THAT ALL THERE IS TO IT?
IT WORKS! I CAN FEEL HIS EARS!
AFTER ALL, POP... YOU'LL HAVE TO ADMIT THAT IT'S A BUNNY!
YEAH, I KNOW...BUT IT AIN'T TH' EATIN' KIND!
BAH!
WR-R-R
WR-R!

Walt Disney's

MICKEY MOUSE in THE MYSTERY OF FREEFER HALL PART 2

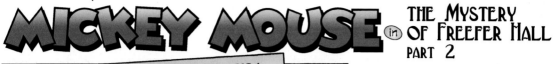

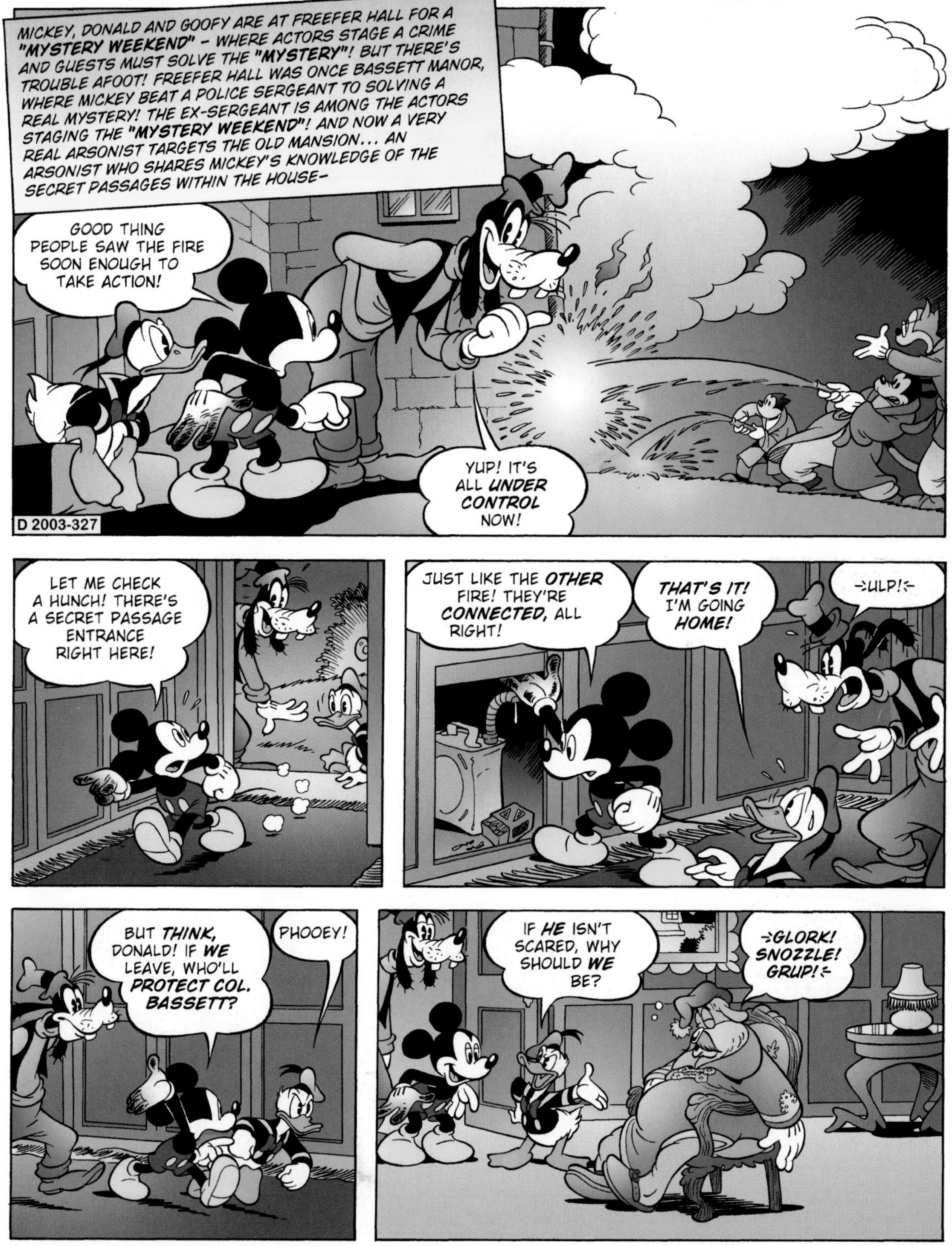
MICKEY, DONALD AND GOOFY ARE AT FREEFER HALL FOR A "MYSTERY WEEKEND" – WHERE ACTORS STAGE A CRIME AND GUESTS MUST SOLVE THE "MYSTERY"! BUT THERE'S TROUBLE AFOOT! FREEFER HALL WAS ONCE BASSETT MANOR, WHERE MICKEY BEAT A POLICE SERGEANT TO SOLVING A REAL MYSTERY! THE EX-SERGEANT IS AMONG THE ACTORS STAGING THE "MYSTERY WEEKEND"! AND NOW A VERY REAL ARSONIST TARGETS THE OLD MANSION... AN ARSONIST WHO SHARES MICKEY'S KNOWLEDGE OF THE SECRET PASSAGES WITHIN THE HOUSE–
GOOD THING PEOPLE SAW THE FIRE SOON ENOUGH TO TAKE ACTION!
YUP! IT'S ALL UNDER CONTROL NOW!
D 2003-327
LET ME CHECK A HUNCH! THERE'S A SECRET PASSAGE ENTRANCE RIGHT HERE!
JUST LIKE THE OTHER FIRE! THEY'RE CONNECTED, ALL RIGHT!
THAT'S IT! I'M GOING HOME!
ULP!
BUT THINK, DONALD! IF WE LEAVE, WHO'LL PROTECT COL. BASSETT?
PHOOEY!
IF HE ISN'T SCARED, WHY SHOULD WE BE?
GLORK! SNOZZLE! GRUP!

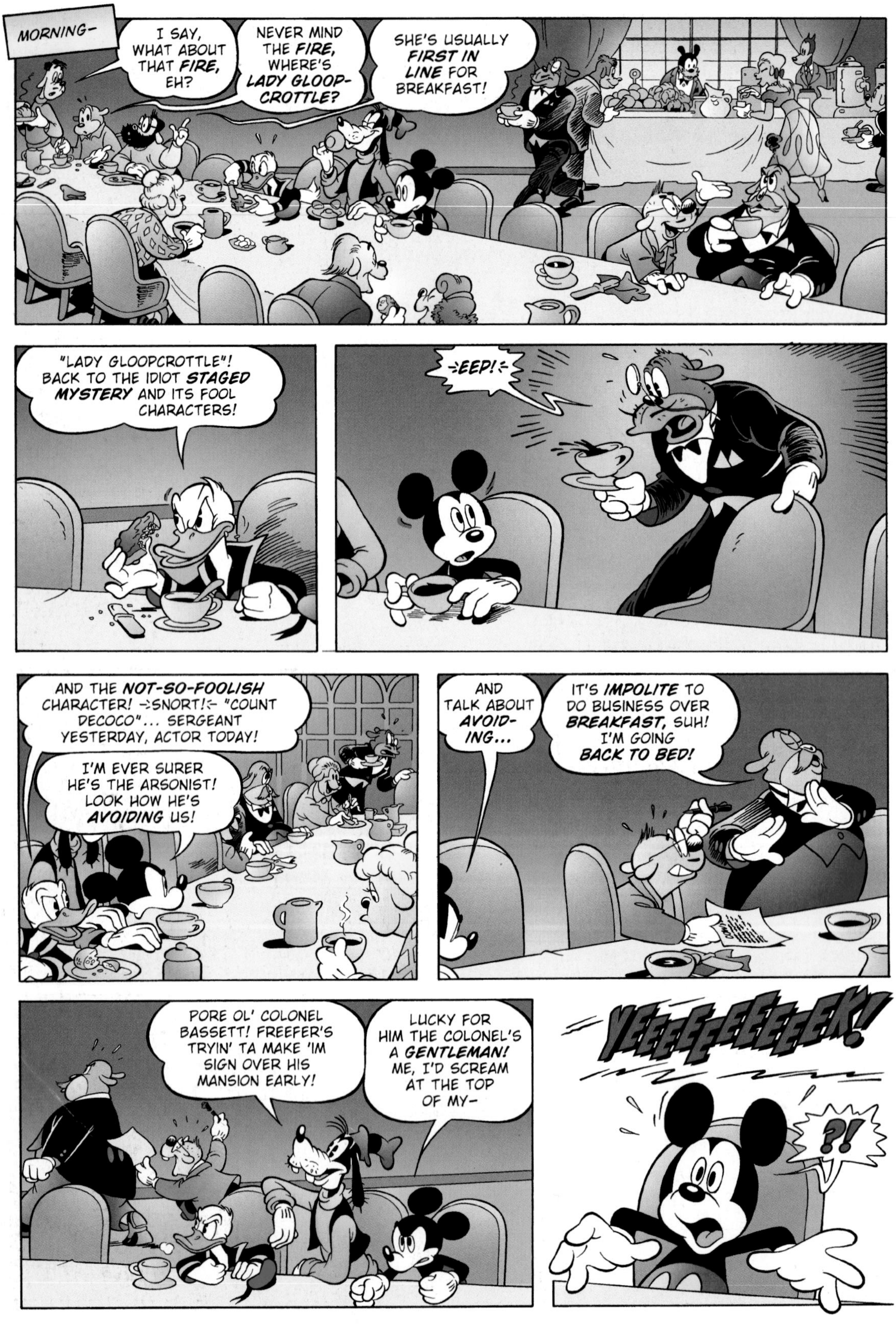
MORNING–
I SAY, WHAT ABOUT THAT *FIRE,* EH?
NEVER MIND THE *FIRE,* WHERE'S *LADY GLOOPCROTTLE?*
SHE'S USUALLY *FIRST IN LINE* FOR BREAKFAST!
"LADY GLOOPCROTTLE"! BACK TO THE IDIOT *STAGED MYSTERY* AND ITS FOOL CHARACTERS!
⇾*EEP!*⇽
AND THE *NOT-SO-FOOLISH* CHARACTER! ⇾SNORT!⇽ "COUNT DECOCO"... SERGEANT YESTERDAY, ACTOR TODAY!
I'M EVER SURER HE'S THE ARSONIST! LOOK HOW HE'S *AVOIDING* US!
AND TALK ABOUT *AVOIDING...*
IT'S *IMPOLITE* TO DO BUSINESS OVER *BREAKFAST,* SUH! I'M GOING *BACK TO BED!*
PORE OL' COLONEL BASSETT! FREEFER'S TRYIN' TA MAKE 'IM SIGN OVER HIS MANSION EARLY!
LUCKY FOR HIM THE COLONEL'S A *GENTLEMAN!* ME, I'D SCREAM AT THE TOP OF MY–
YEEEEEEEEEEK!
?!

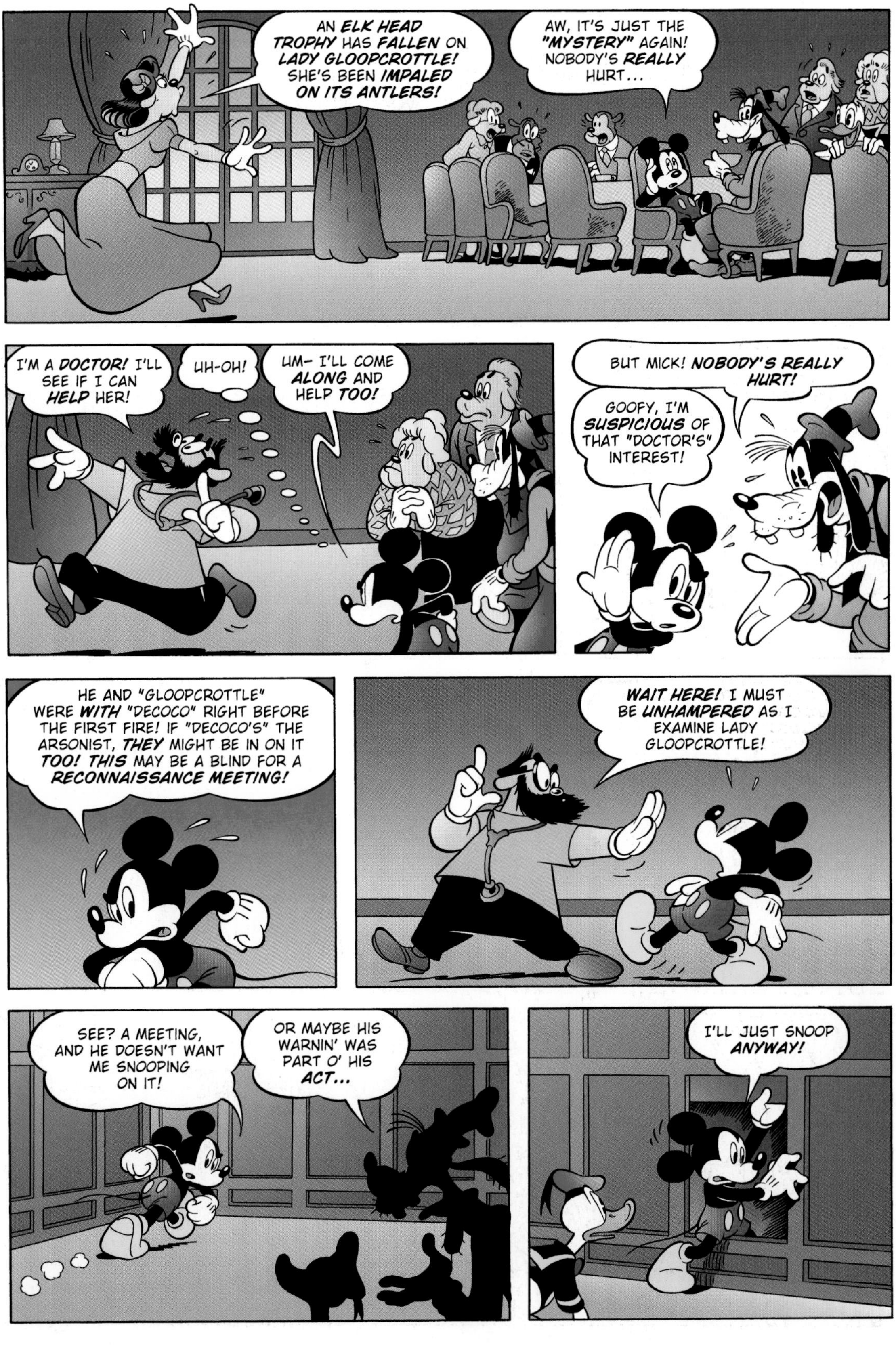
AN ELK HEAD TROPHY HAS FALLEN ON LADY GLOOPCROTTLE! SHE'S BEEN IMPALED ON ITS ANTLERS!
AW, IT'S JUST THE "MYSTERY" AGAIN! NOBODY'S REALLY HURT...
I'M A DOCTOR! I'LL SEE IF I CAN HELP HER!
UH-OH!
UM– I'LL COME ALONG AND HELP TOO!
BUT MICK! NOBODY'S REALLY HURT!
GOOFY, I'M SUSPICIOUS OF THAT "DOCTOR'S" INTEREST!
HE AND "GLOOPCROTTLE" WERE WITH "DECOCO" RIGHT BEFORE THE FIRST FIRE! IF "DECOCO'S" THE ARSONIST, THEY MIGHT BE IN ON IT TOO! THIS MAY BE A BLIND FOR A RECONNAISSANCE MEETING!
WAIT HERE! I MUST BE UNHAMPERED AS I EXAMINE LADY GLOOPCROTTLE!
SEE? A MEETING, AND HE DOESN'T WANT ME SNOOPING ON IT!
OR MAYBE HIS WARNIN' WAS PART O' HIS ACT...
I'LL JUST SNOOP ANYWAY!

I'LL CATCH THE "DOCTOR" AND "GLOOPCROTTLE" MID-CONSPIRACY AND *MAKE* 'EM SPILL THE BEANS! THEY—

WHAT? OH, IT'S *YOU*, IS IT? WHAT ARE *YOU* DOING HERE?

HUH? WHERE'S "GLOOPCROTTLE"?

YOU'RE SNOOPING BEHIND THE SCENERY, YOUNG MAN! THE *ACTRESS* PLAYING LADY GLOOPCROTTLE WENT HOME LAST NIGHT!

∹ULP!∹

IN A MOMENT I'LL ANNOUNCE HER *CHARACTER* HAS BEEN "MURDERED"! ANY QUESTIONS?

ER, UH... *NO!*

∹SIGH!∹ OKAY, SO I GOT CARRIED AWAY!

∹HUH?∹ WHAT'S *THIS?*

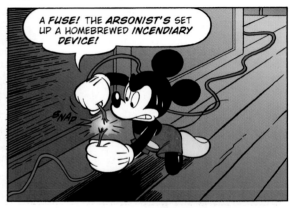

A *FUSE!* THE *ARSONIST'S* SET UP A HOMEBREWED *INCENDIARY DEVICE!*

SNAP

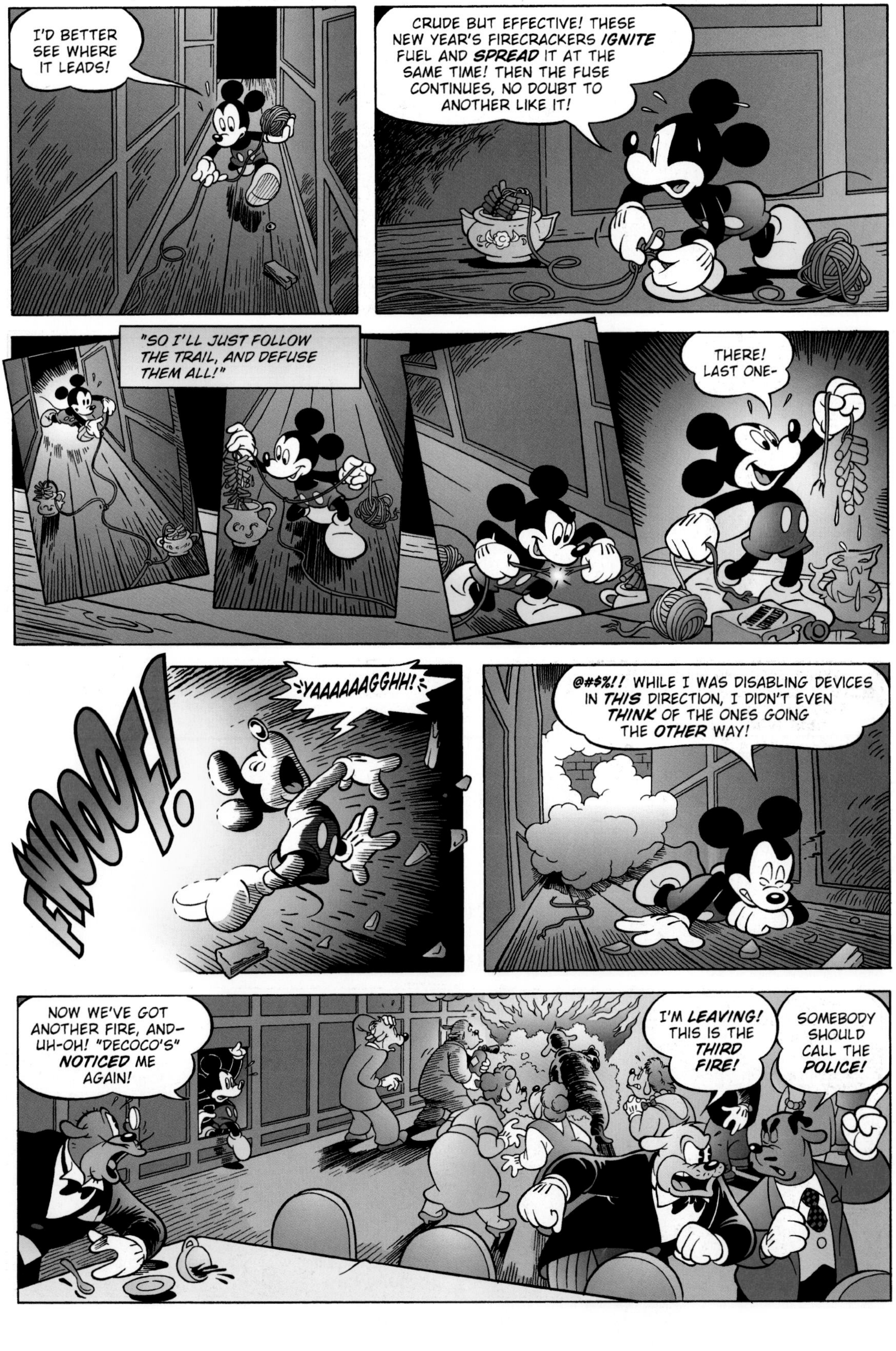
I'D BETTER SEE WHERE IT LEADS!
CRUDE BUT EFFECTIVE! THESE NEW YEAR'S FIRECRACKERS IGNITE FUEL AND SPREAD IT AT THE SAME TIME! THEN THE FUSE CONTINUES, NO DOUBT TO ANOTHER LIKE IT!
"SO I'LL JUST FOLLOW THE TRAIL, AND DEFUSE THEM ALL!"
THERE! LAST ONE-
FWOOOF!
YAAAAAAGGHH!
@#$%!! WHILE I WAS DISABLING DEVICES IN THIS DIRECTION, I DIDN'T EVEN THINK OF THE ONES GOING THE OTHER WAY!
NOW WE'VE GOT ANOTHER FIRE, AND— UH-OH! "DECOCO'S" NOTICED ME AGAIN!
I'M LEAVING! THIS IS THE THIRD FIRE!
SOMEBODY SHOULD CALL THE POLICE!

HE'S ESCAPING INTO A SECRET PASSAGE! DOGGONE, THAT *CLINCHES* IT!

DONALD! GOOFY! GET "DECOCO"! HE DID IT!

AND HE COULDA TAKEN ANY ONE OF THESE PATHS! WE'LL HAVE TO *SPLIT UP!*

OKAY, MICK!

IT'S AGAINST MY BETTER JUDGMENT— BUT ALL RIGHT!

I JUST HOPE *ONE* OF US CATCHES HIM BEFORE HE *STARTS* ANY MORE *FIRES!*

DO I HEAR *FOOT- STEPS* AHEAD?

GLUMP

GLUMP

~URK!~

GOTCHA!

ALL RIGHT! YOU'VE GOT ME! I'LL CONFESS!

SWELL! LET'S HEAR IT!

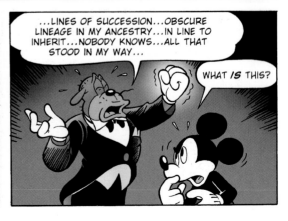

...LINES OF SUCCESSION...OBSCURE LINEAGE IN MY ANCESTRY...IN LINE TO INHERIT...NOBODY KNOWS...ALL THAT STOOD IN MY WAY...

WHAT *IS* THIS?

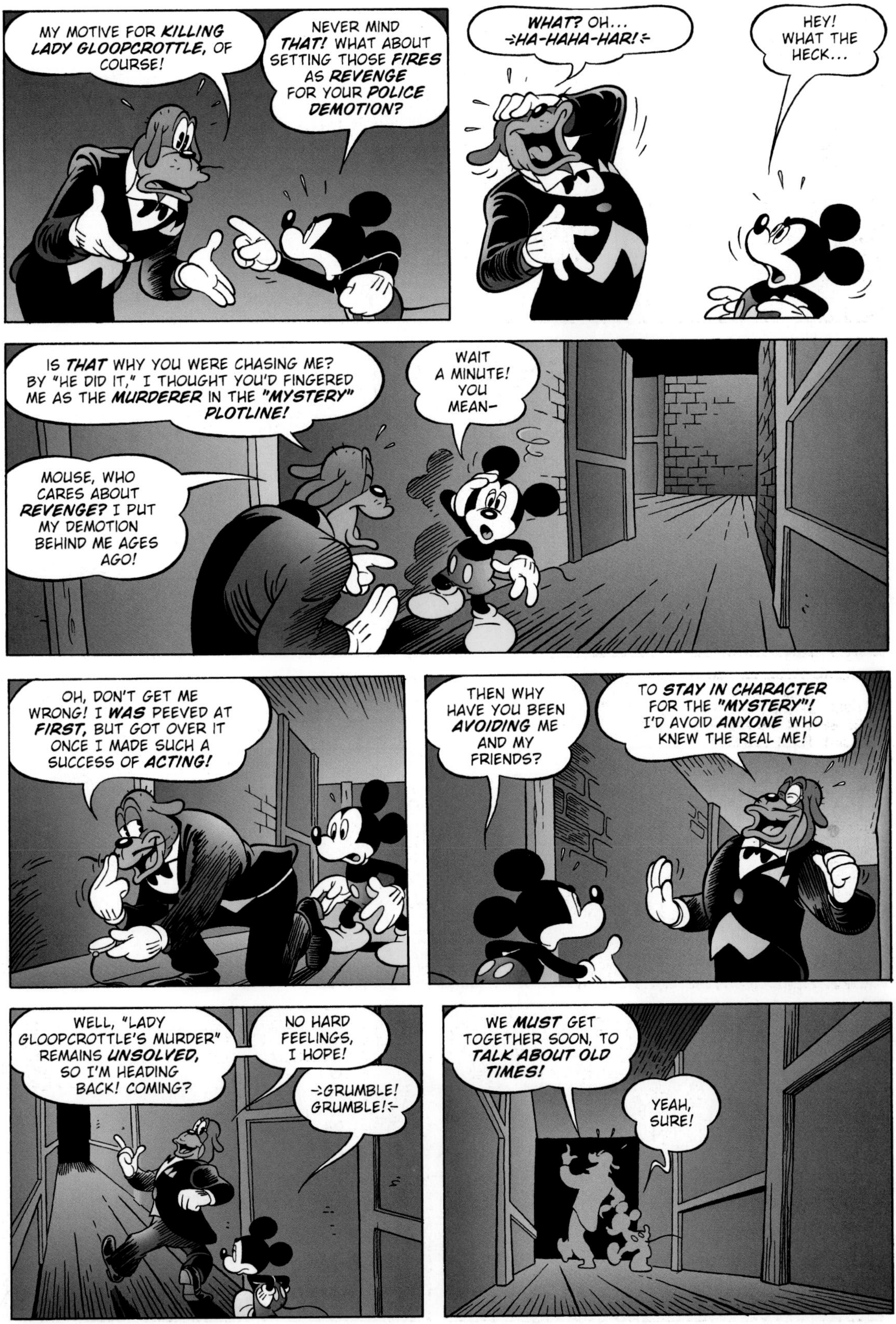
MY MOTIVE FOR KILLING LADY GLOOPCROTTLE, OF COURSE!
NEVER MIND THAT! WHAT ABOUT SETTING THOSE FIRES AS REVENGE FOR YOUR POLICE DEMOTION?
WHAT? OH... HA-HAHA-HAR!
HEY! WHAT THE HECK...
IS THAT WHY YOU WERE CHASING ME? BY "HE DID IT," I THOUGHT YOU'D FINGERED ME AS THE MURDERER IN THE "MYSTERY" PLOTLINE!
WAIT A MINUTE! YOU MEAN-
MOUSE, WHO CARES ABOUT REVENGE? I PUT MY DEMOTION BEHIND ME AGES AGO!
OH, DON'T GET ME WRONG! I WAS PEEVED AT FIRST, BUT GOT OVER IT ONCE I MADE SUCH A SUCCESS OF ACTING!
THEN WHY HAVE YOU BEEN AVOIDING ME AND MY FRIENDS?
TO STAY IN CHARACTER FOR THE "MYSTERY"! I'D AVOID ANYONE WHO KNEW THE REAL ME!
WELL, "LADY GLOOPCROTTLE'S MURDER" REMAINS UNSOLVED, SO I'M HEADING BACK! COMING?
NO HARD FEELINGS, I HOPE!
GRUMBLE! GRUMBLE!
WE MUST GET TOGETHER SOON, TO TALK ABOUT OLD TIMES!
YEAH, SURE!

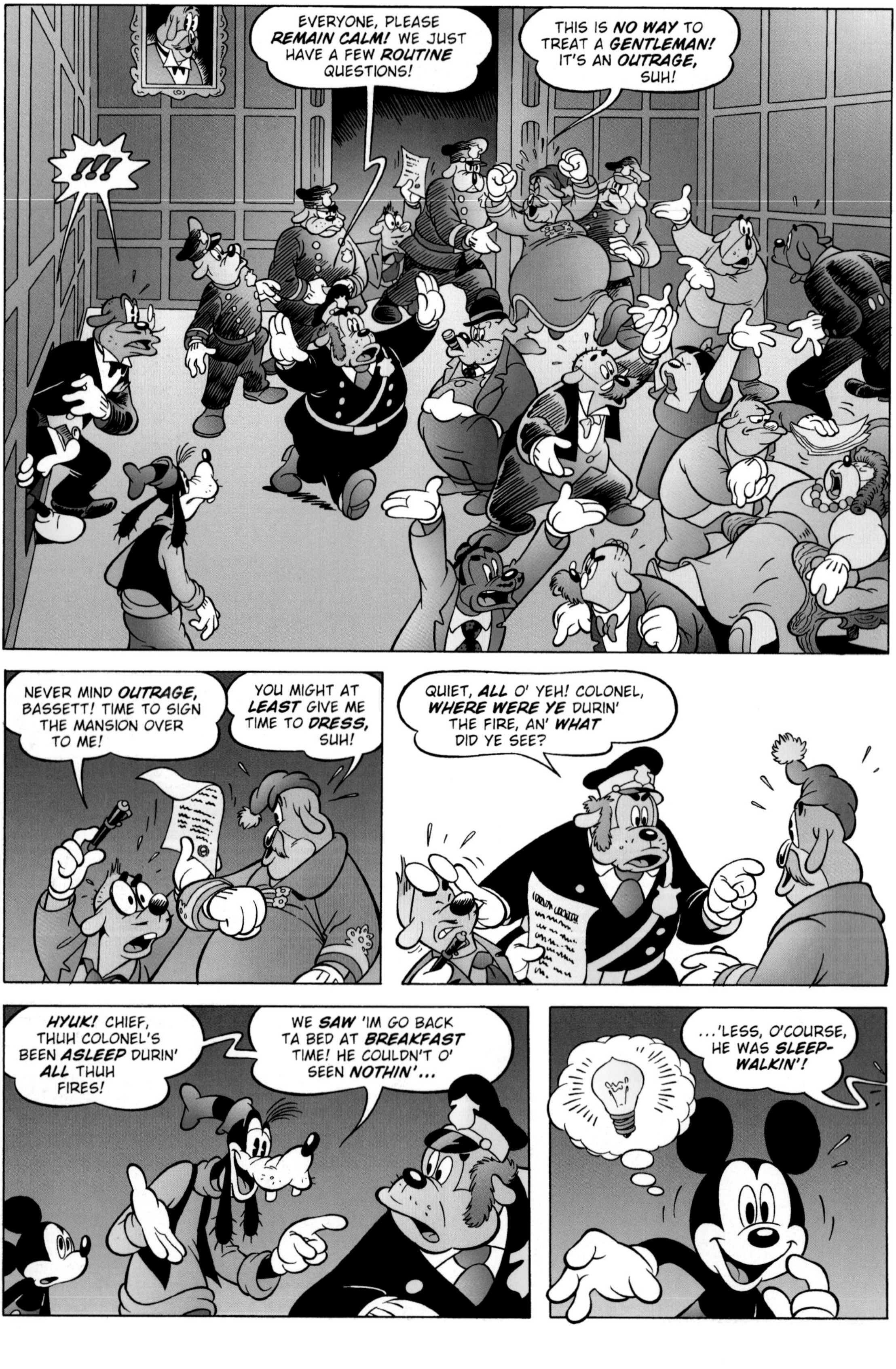
!!!
EVERYONE, PLEASE REMAIN CALM! WE JUST HAVE A FEW ROUTINE QUESTIONS!
THIS IS NO WAY TO TREAT A GENTLEMAN! IT'S AN OUTRAGE, SUH!
NEVER MIND OUTRAGE, BASSETT! TIME TO SIGN THE MANSION OVER TO ME!
YOU MIGHT AT LEAST GIVE ME TIME TO DRESS, SUH!
QUIET, ALL O' YEH! COLONEL, WHERE WERE YE DURIN' THE FIRE, AN' WHAT DID YE SEE?
HYUK! CHIEF, THUH COLONEL'S BEEN ASLEEP DURIN' ALL THUH FIRES!
WE SAW 'IM GO BACK TA BED AT BREAKFAST TIME! HE COULDN'T O' SEEN NOTHIN'...
...'LESS, O'COURSE, HE WAS SLEEP-WALKIN'!

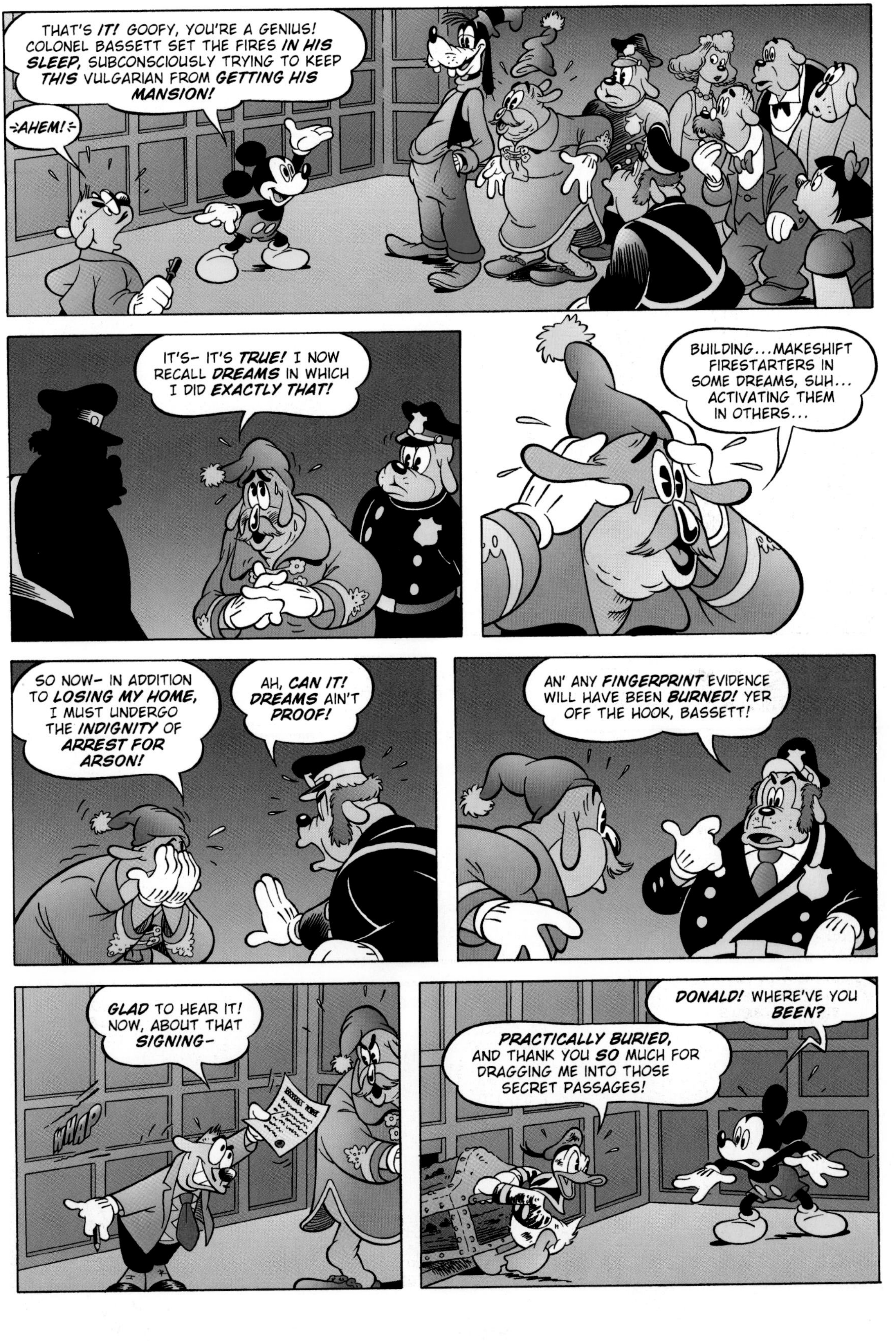

THAT'S IT! GOOFY, YOU'RE A GENIUS! COLONEL BASSETT SET THE FIRES IN HIS SLEEP, SUBCONSCIOUSLY TRYING TO KEEP THIS VULGARIAN FROM GETTING HIS MANSION!
AHEM!
IT'S- IT'S TRUE! I NOW RECALL DREAMS IN WHICH I DID EXACTLY THAT!
BUILDING...MAKESHIFT FIRESTARTERS IN SOME DREAMS, SUH... ACTIVATING THEM IN OTHERS...
SO NOW- IN ADDITION TO LOSING MY HOME, I MUST UNDERGO THE INDIGNITY OF ARREST FOR ARSON!
AH, CAN IT! DREAMS AIN'T PROOF!
AN' ANY FINGERPRINT EVIDENCE WILL HAVE BEEN BURNED! YER OFF THE HOOK, BASSETT!
GLAD TO HEAR IT! NOW, ABOUT THAT SIGNING-
WHAP
DONALD! WHERE'VE YOU BEEN?
PRACTICALLY BURIED, AND THANK YOU SO MUCH FOR DRAGGING ME INTO THOSE SECRET PASSAGES!

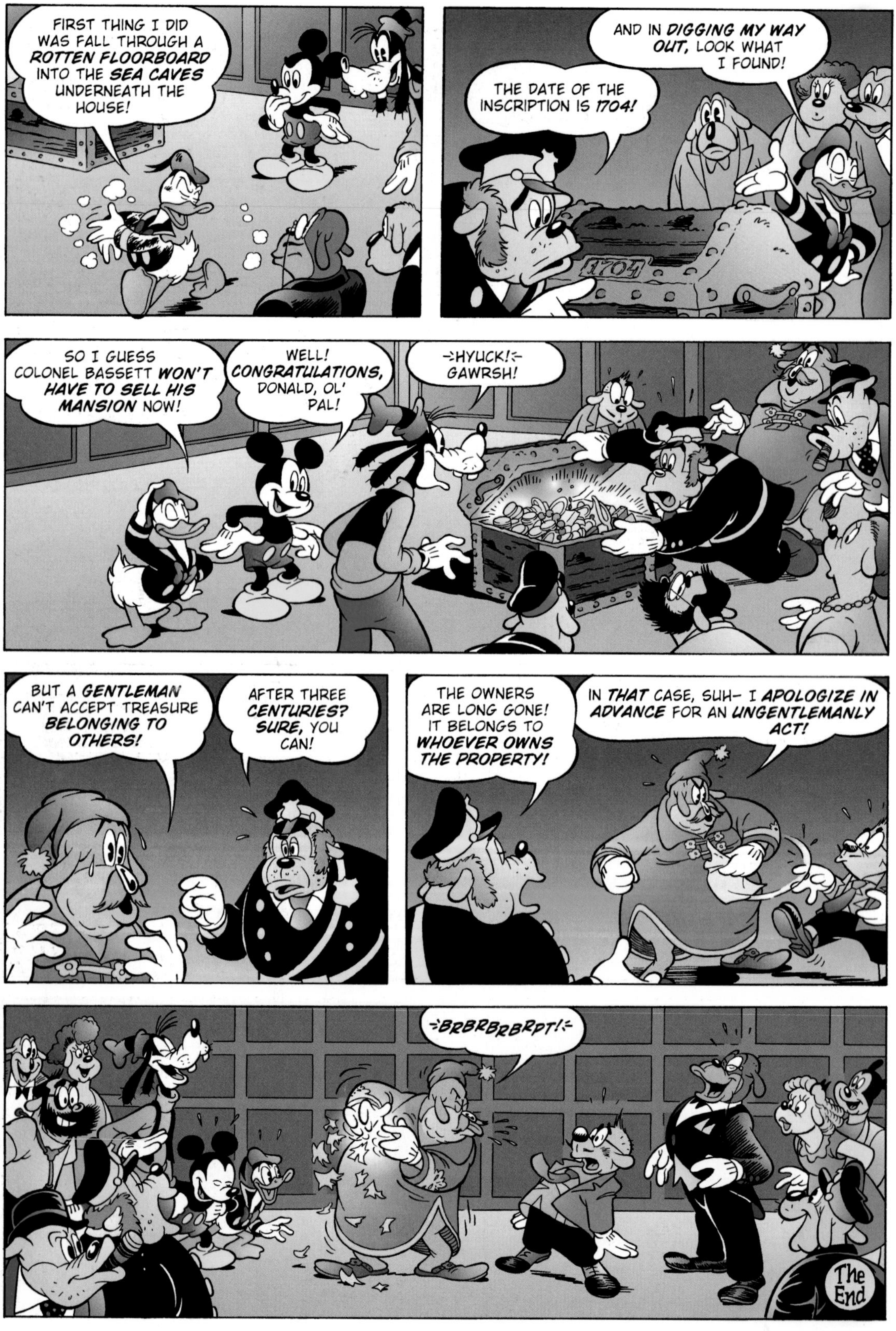
FIRST THING I DID WAS FALL THROUGH A ROTTEN FLOORBOARD INTO THE SEA CAVES UNDERNEATH THE HOUSE!
AND IN DIGGING MY WAY OUT, LOOK WHAT I FOUND!
THE DATE OF THE INSCRIPTION IS 1704!
1704
SO I GUESS COLONEL BASSETT WON'T HAVE TO SELL HIS MANSION NOW!
WELL! CONGRATULATIONS, DONALD, OL' PAL!
HYUCK! GAWRSH!
BUT A GENTLEMAN CAN'T ACCEPT TREASURE BELONGING TO OTHERS!
AFTER THREE CENTURIES? SURE, YOU CAN!
THE OWNERS ARE LONG GONE! IT BELONGS TO WHOEVER OWNS THE PROPERTY!
IN THAT CASE, SUH– I APOLOGIZE IN ADVANCE FOR AN UNGENTLEMANLY ACT!
BRBRBRBRBRPT!
The End

Walt Disney's Donald Duck in ORNERY ORB

PART 3 OF THE ORB SAGA

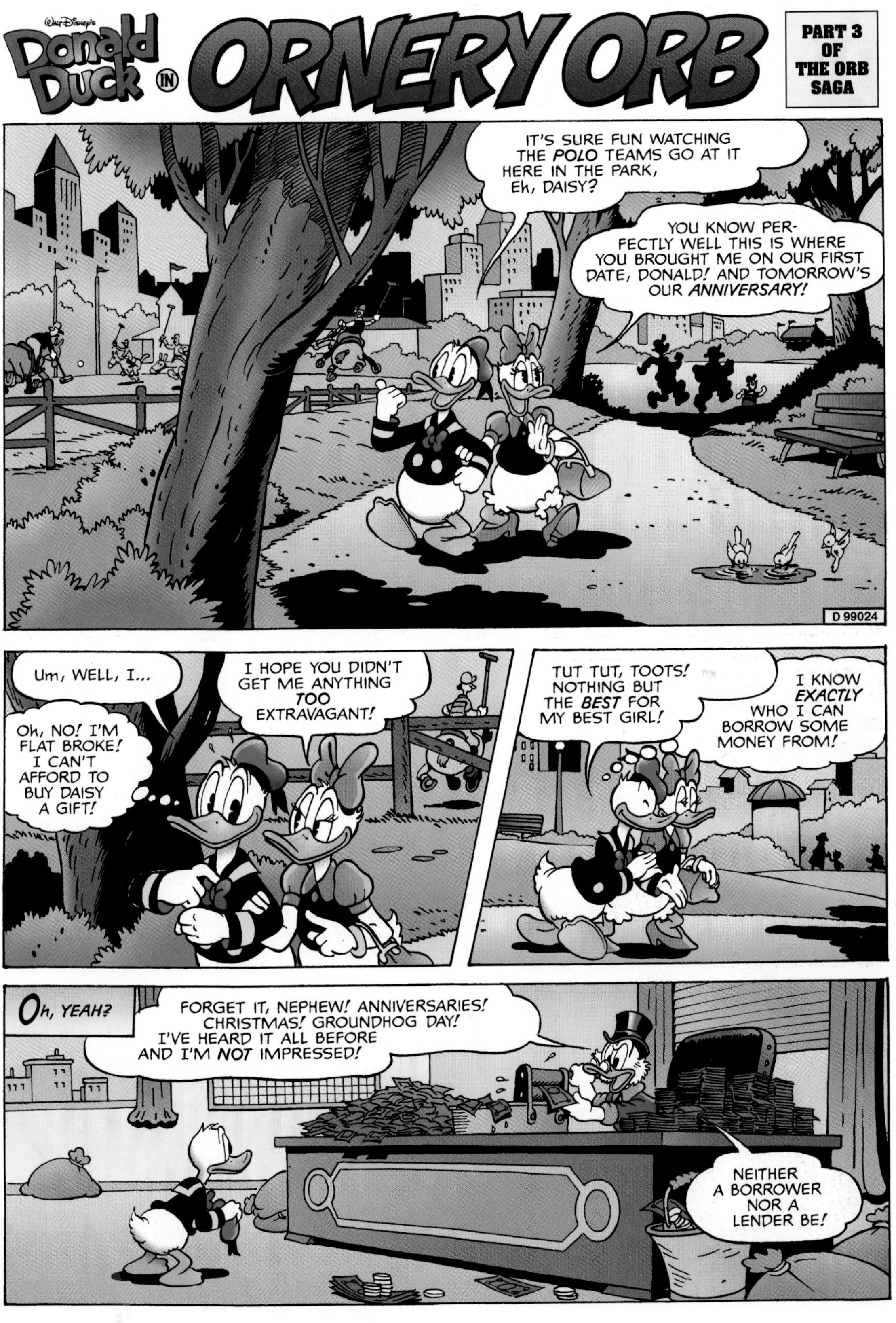

IT'S SURE FUN WATCHING THE *POLO* TEAMS GO AT IT HERE IN THE PARK, Eh, DAISY?
YOU KNOW PER-FECTLY WELL THIS IS WHERE YOU BROUGHT ME ON OUR FIRST DATE, DONALD! AND TOMORROW'S OUR *ANNIVERSARY!*
D 99024
Um, WELL, I...
I HOPE YOU DIDN'T GET ME ANYTHING *TOO* EXTRAVAGANT!
Oh, NO! I'M FLAT BROKE! I CAN'T AFFORD TO BUY DAISY A GIFT!
TUT TUT, TOOTS! NOTHING BUT THE *BEST* FOR MY BEST GIRL!
I KNOW *EXACTLY* WHO I CAN BORROW SOME MONEY FROM!
Oh, YEAH?
FORGET IT, NEPHEW! ANNIVERSARIES! CHRISTMAS! GROUNDHOG DAY! I'VE HEARD IT ALL BEFORE AND I'M *NOT* IMPRESSED!
NEITHER A BORROWER NOR A LENDER BE!

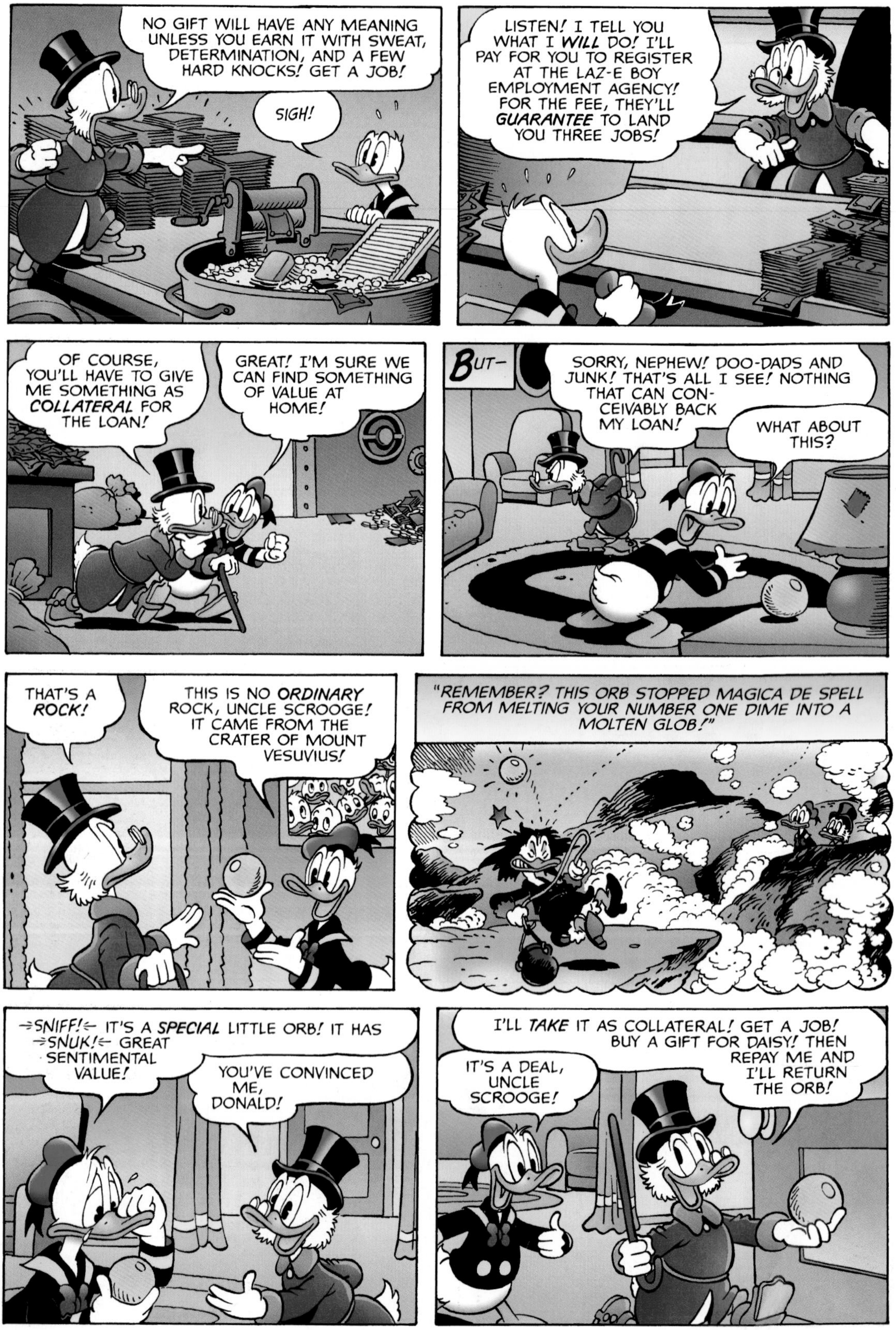
NO GIFT WILL HAVE ANY MEANING UNLESS YOU EARN IT WITH SWEAT, DETERMINATION, AND A FEW HARD KNOCKS! GET A JOB!
SIGH!
LISTEN! I TELL YOU WHAT I WILL DO! I'LL PAY FOR YOU TO REGISTER AT THE LAZ-E BOY EMPLOYMENT AGENCY! FOR THE FEE, THEY'LL GUARANTEE TO LAND YOU THREE JOBS!
OF COURSE, YOU'LL HAVE TO GIVE ME SOMETHING AS COLLATERAL FOR THE LOAN!
GREAT! I'M SURE WE CAN FIND SOMETHING OF VALUE AT HOME!
BUT—
SORRY, NEPHEW! DOO-DADS AND JUNK! THAT'S ALL I SEE! NOTHING THAT CAN CONCEIVABLY BACK MY LOAN!
WHAT ABOUT THIS?
THAT'S A ROCK!
THIS IS NO ORDINARY ROCK, UNCLE SCROOGE! IT CAME FROM THE CRATER OF MOUNT VESUVIUS!
"REMEMBER? THIS ORB STOPPED MAGICA DE SPELL FROM MELTING YOUR NUMBER ONE DIME INTO A MOLTEN GLOB!"
⇒SNIFF!⇐ IT'S A SPECIAL LITTLE ORB! IT HAS ⇒SNUK!⇐ GREAT SENTIMENTAL VALUE!
YOU'VE CONVINCED ME, DONALD!
I'LL TAKE IT AS COLLATERAL! GET A JOB! BUY A GIFT FOR DAISY! THEN REPAY ME AND I'LL RETURN THE ORB!
IT'S A DEAL, UNCLE SCROOGE!

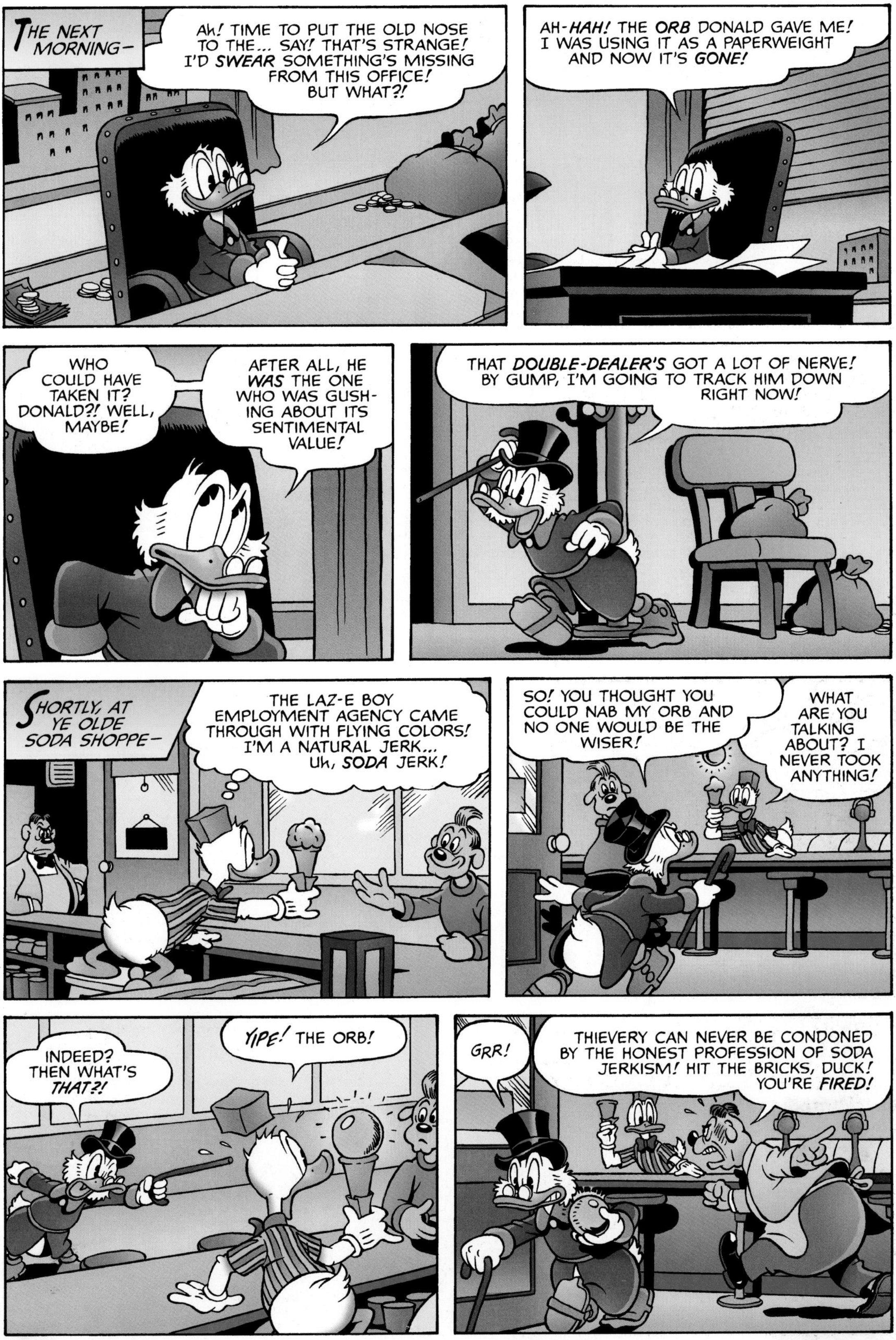

THE NEXT MORNING—
Ah! TIME TO PUT THE OLD NOSE TO THE... SAY! THAT'S STRANGE! I'D SWEAR SOMETHING'S MISSING FROM THIS OFFICE! BUT WHAT?!
AH-HAH! THE ORB DONALD GAVE ME! I WAS USING IT AS A PAPERWEIGHT AND NOW IT'S GONE!
WHO COULD HAVE TAKEN IT? DONALD?! WELL, MAYBE!
AFTER ALL, HE WAS THE ONE WHO WAS GUSHING ABOUT ITS SENTIMENTAL VALUE!
THAT DOUBLE-DEALER'S GOT A LOT OF NERVE! BY GUMP, I'M GOING TO TRACK HIM DOWN RIGHT NOW!
SHORTLY, AT YE OLDE SODA SHOPPE—
THE LAZ-E BOY EMPLOYMENT AGENCY CAME THROUGH WITH FLYING COLORS! I'M A NATURAL JERK... Uh, SODA JERK!
SO! YOU THOUGHT YOU COULD NAB MY ORB AND NO ONE WOULD BE THE WISER!
WHAT ARE YOU TALKING ABOUT? I NEVER TOOK ANYTHING!
INDEED? THEN WHAT'S THAT?!
YIPE! THE ORB!
GRR!
THIEVERY CAN NEVER BE CONDONED BY THE HONEST PROFESSION OF SODA JERKISM! HIT THE BRICKS, DUCK! YOU'RE FIRED!

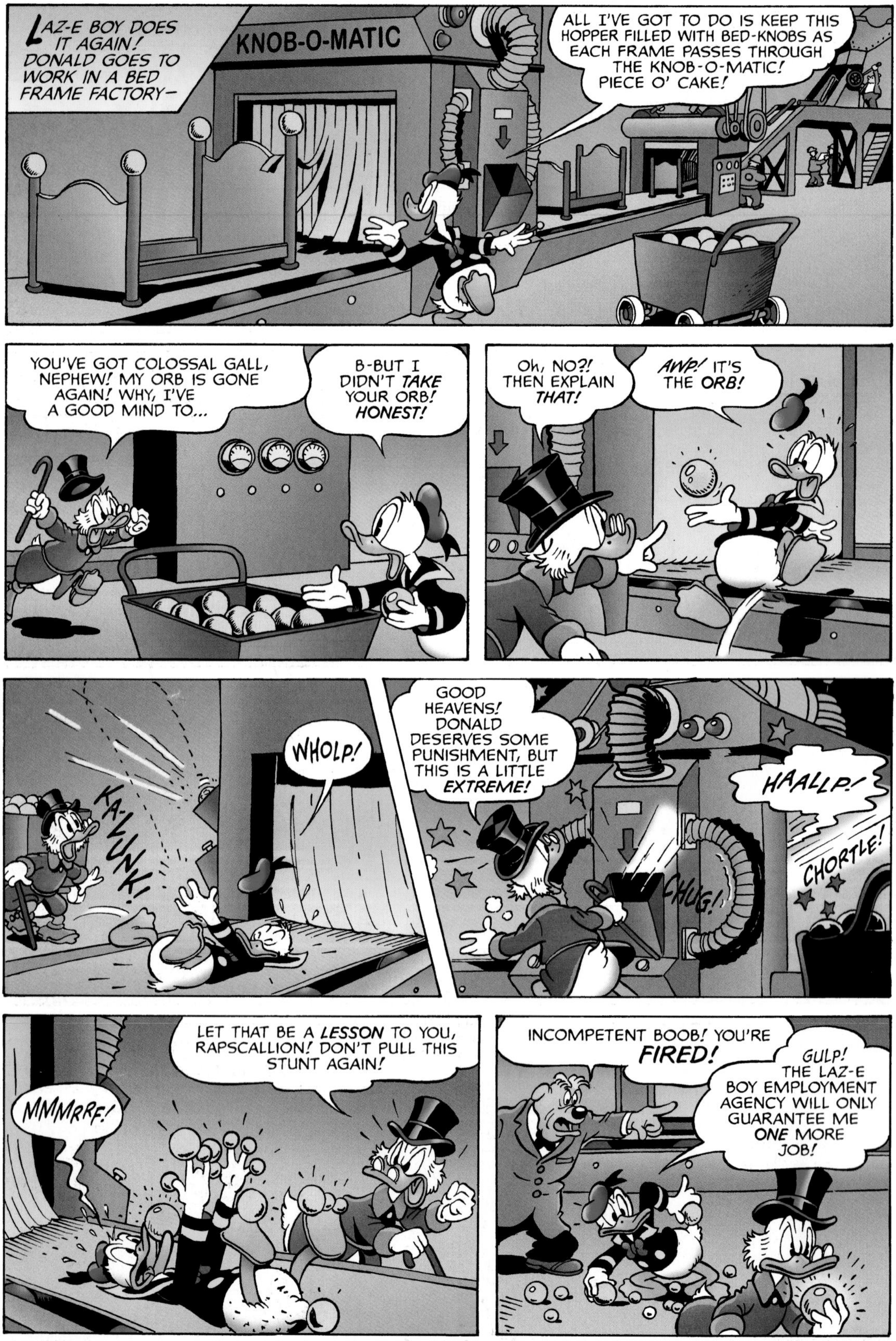
LAZ-E BOY DOES IT AGAIN! DONALD GOES TO WORK IN A BED FRAME FACTORY—
KNOB-O-MATIC
ALL I'VE GOT TO DO IS KEEP THIS HOPPER FILLED WITH BED-KNOBS AS EACH FRAME PASSES THROUGH THE KNOB-O-MATIC! PIECE O' CAKE!
YOU'VE GOT COLOSSAL GALL, NEPHEW! MY ORB IS GONE AGAIN! WHY, I'VE A GOOD MIND TO...
B-BUT I DIDN'T TAKE YOUR ORB! HONEST!
Oh, NO?! THEN EXPLAIN THAT!
AWP! IT'S THE ORB!
KA-VUNK!
WHOLP!
GOOD HEAVENS! DONALD DESERVES SOME PUNISHMENT, BUT THIS IS A LITTLE EXTREME!
HAALLP!
CHUG!
CHORTLE!
MMMRRF!
LET THAT BE A LESSON TO YOU, RAPSCALLION! DON'T PULL THIS STUNT AGAIN!
INCOMPETENT BOOB! YOU'RE FIRED!
GULP! THE LAZ-E BOY EMPLOYMENT AGENCY WILL ONLY GUARANTEE ME ONE MORE JOB!

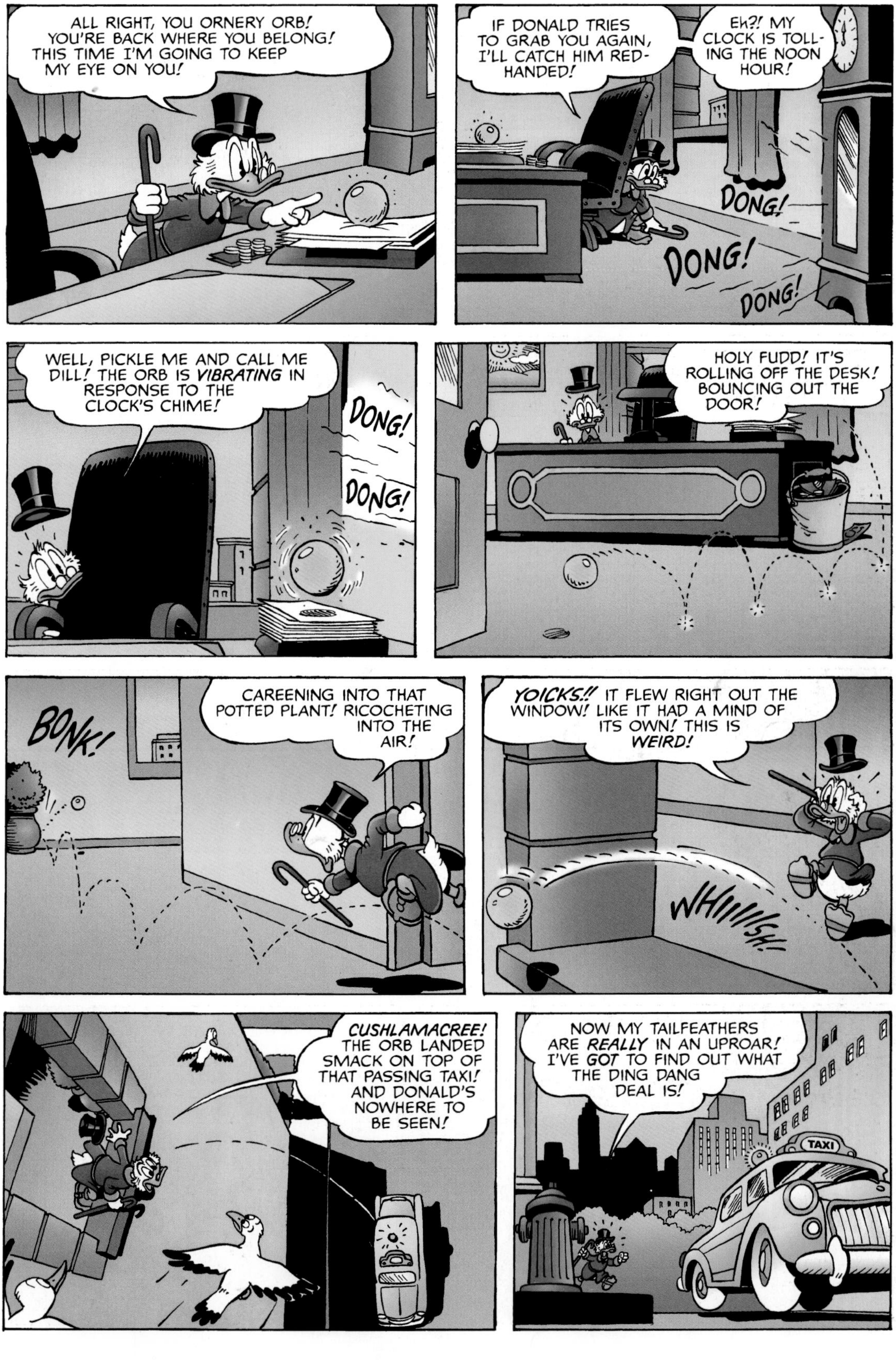
ALL RIGHT, YOU ORNERY ORB! YOU'RE BACK WHERE YOU BELONG! THIS TIME I'M GOING TO KEEP MY EYE ON YOU!
IF DONALD TRIES TO GRAB YOU AGAIN, I'LL CATCH HIM RED-HANDED!
EH?! MY CLOCK IS TOLLING THE NOON HOUR!
DONG!
DONG!
DONG!
WELL, PICKLE ME AND CALL ME DILL! THE ORB IS VIBRATING IN RESPONSE TO THE CLOCK'S CHIME!
DONG!
DONG!
HOLY FUDD! IT'S ROLLING OFF THE DESK! BOUNCING OUT THE DOOR!
BONK!
CAREENING INTO THAT POTTED PLANT! RICOCHETING INTO THE AIR!
YOICKS!! IT FLEW RIGHT OUT THE WINDOW! LIKE IT HAD A MIND OF ITS OWN! THIS IS WEIRD!
WHIIIISH!
CUSHLAMACREE! THE ORB LANDED SMACK ON TOP OF THAT PASSING TAXI! AND DONALD'S NOWHERE TO BE SEEN!
NOW MY TAILFEATHERS ARE REALLY IN AN UPROAR! I'VE GOT TO FIND OUT WHAT THE DING DANG DEAL IS!
TAXI

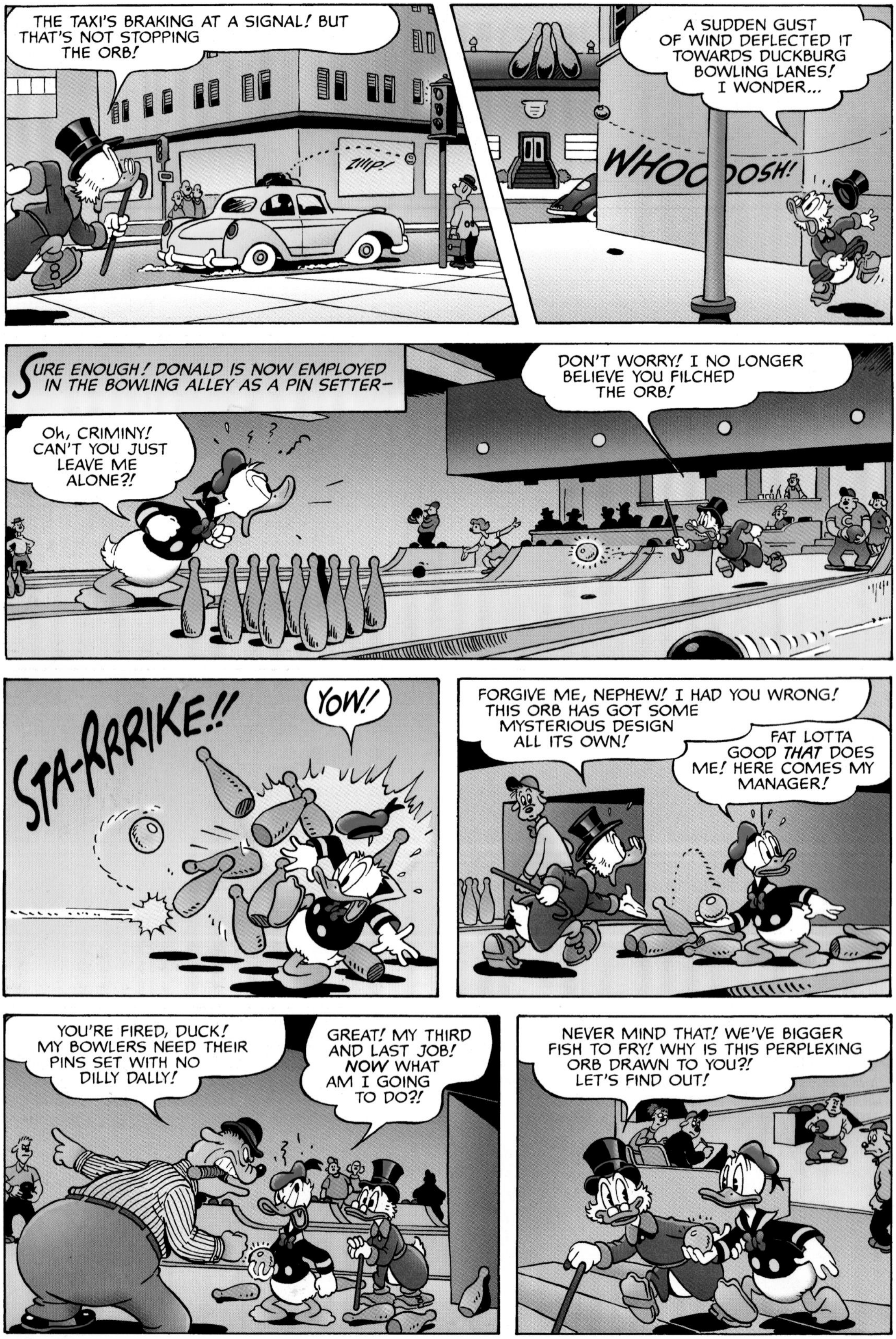
THE TAXI'S BRAKING AT A SIGNAL! BUT THAT'S NOT STOPPING THE ORB!
ZLIP!
A SUDDEN GUST OF WIND DEFLECTED IT TOWARDS DUCKBURG BOWLING LANES! I WONDER...
WHOOOOSH!
SURE ENOUGH! DONALD IS NOW EMPLOYED IN THE BOWLING ALLEY AS A PIN SETTER–
Oh, CRIMINY! CAN'T YOU JUST LEAVE ME ALONE?!
DON'T WORRY! I NO LONGER BELIEVE YOU FILCHED THE ORB!
STA-RRRIKE!!
YOW!
FORGIVE ME, NEPHEW! I HAD YOU WRONG! THIS ORB HAS GOT SOME MYSTERIOUS DESIGN ALL ITS OWN!
FAT LOTTA GOOD THAT DOES ME! HERE COMES MY MANAGER!
YOU'RE FIRED, DUCK! MY BOWLERS NEED THEIR PINS SET WITH NO DILLY DALLY!
GREAT! MY THIRD AND LAST JOB! NOW WHAT AM I GOING TO DO?!
NEVER MIND THAT! WE'VE BIGGER FISH TO FRY! WHY IS THIS PERPLEXING ORB DRAWN TO YOU?! LET'S FIND OUT!

GENTLEMEN, I CAN'T TELL YOU *WHAT* THIS IS! BUT I *CAN* TELL YOU THAT IT IS VERY OLD... ANCIENT, IN FACT!

DUCKBURG UNIVERSITY
HALL OF ANTHROPOLOGY

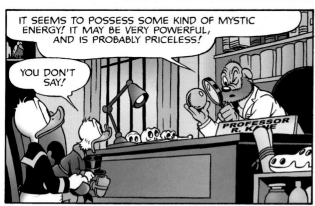

IT SEEMS TO POSSESS SOME KIND OF MYSTIC ENERGY! IT MAY BE VERY POWERFUL, AND IS PROBABLY PRICELESS!

YOU DON'T SAY!

PROFESSOR R. KANE

AND, FOR SOME *UNFATHOMABLE* REASON, THIS OBJECT IS VERY ATTRACTED TO *YOU*, MR. DUCK!

ME?!

IT MAY BE ATTRACTED TO YOU, BUT IT'S *MY* COLLATERAL! AND I'M KEEPING IT UNTIL YOU PAY BACK THE LOAN!

BUT, UNCLE SCROOGE...

I'VE LOST THREE JOBS! THAT'S ALL LAZ-E BOY PROVIDES!

PHONE

WHAT AM I GOING TO DO? I'M IN DEBT TO UNCLE SCROOGE AND I *STILL* CAN'T AFFORD AN ANNIVERSARY GIFT FOR DAISY!

THERE'S NOTHING I *CAN* DO BUT BREAK THE NEWS TO HER! I'LL ASK HER TO MEET ME IN THE PARK! MAYBE SOME PLEASANT SCENERY WILL SOFTEN HER UP!

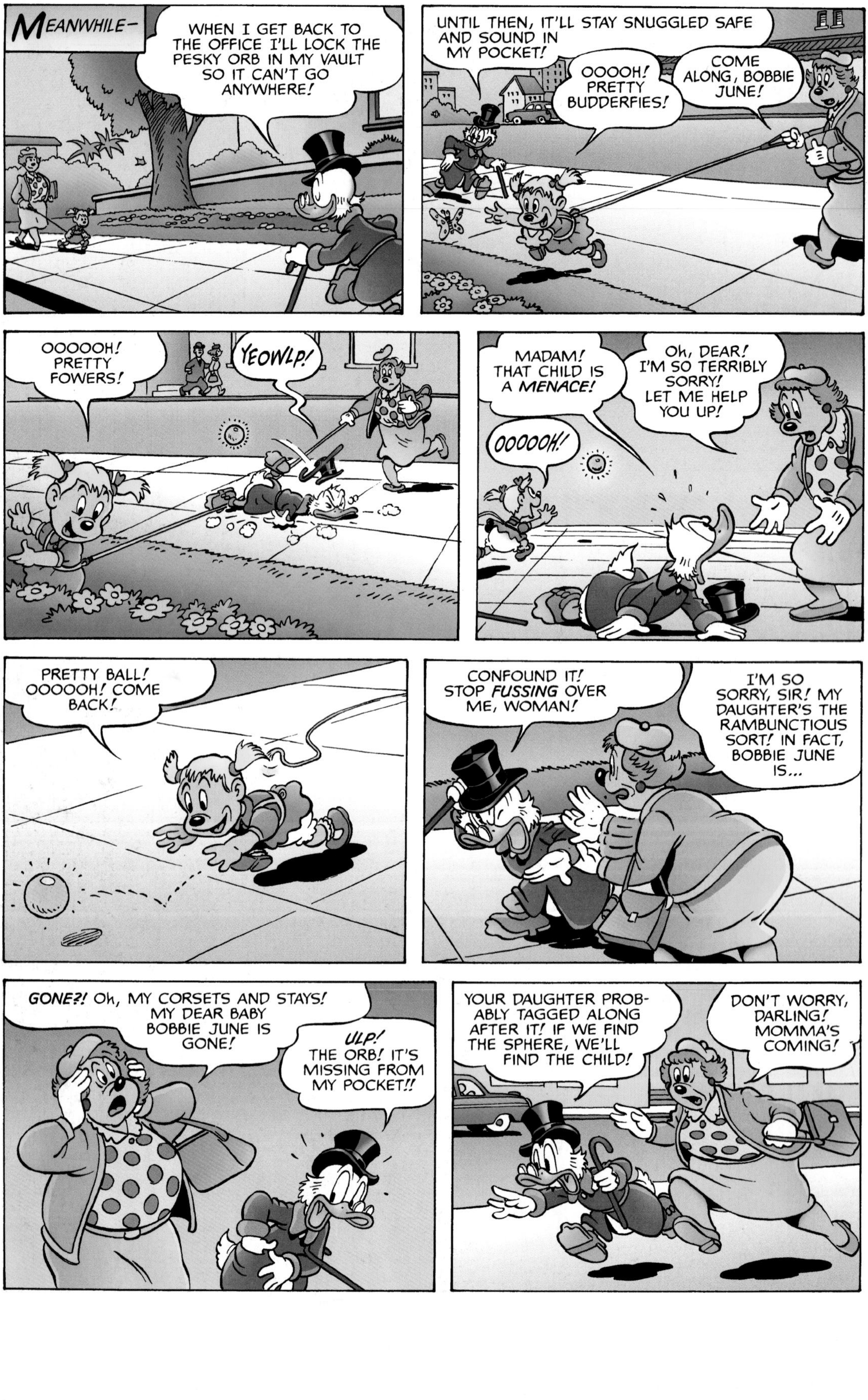
MEANWHILE–
WHEN I GET BACK TO THE OFFICE I'LL LOCK THE PESKY ORB IN MY VAULT SO IT CAN'T GO ANYWHERE!
UNTIL THEN, IT'LL STAY SNUGGLED SAFE AND SOUND IN MY POCKET!
OOOOH! PRETTY BUDDERFIES!
COME ALONG, BOBBIE JUNE!
OOOOOH! PRETTY FOWERS!
YEOWLP!
MADAM! THAT CHILD IS A MENACE!
OOOOOH!
Oh, DEAR! I'M SO TERRIBLY SORRY! LET ME HELP YOU UP!
PRETTY BALL! OOOOOH! COME BACK!
CONFOUND IT! STOP FUSSING OVER ME, WOMAN!
I'M SO SORRY, SIR! MY DAUGHTER'S THE RAMBUNCTIOUS SORT! IN FACT, BOBBIE JUNE IS...
GONE?! Oh, MY CORSETS AND STAYS! MY DEAR BABY BOBBIE JUNE IS GONE!
ULP! THE ORB! IT'S MISSING FROM MY POCKET!!
YOUR DAUGHTER PROBABLY TAGGED ALONG AFTER IT! IF WE FIND THE SPHERE, WE'LL FIND THE CHILD!
DON'T WORRY, DARLING! MOMMA'S COMING!

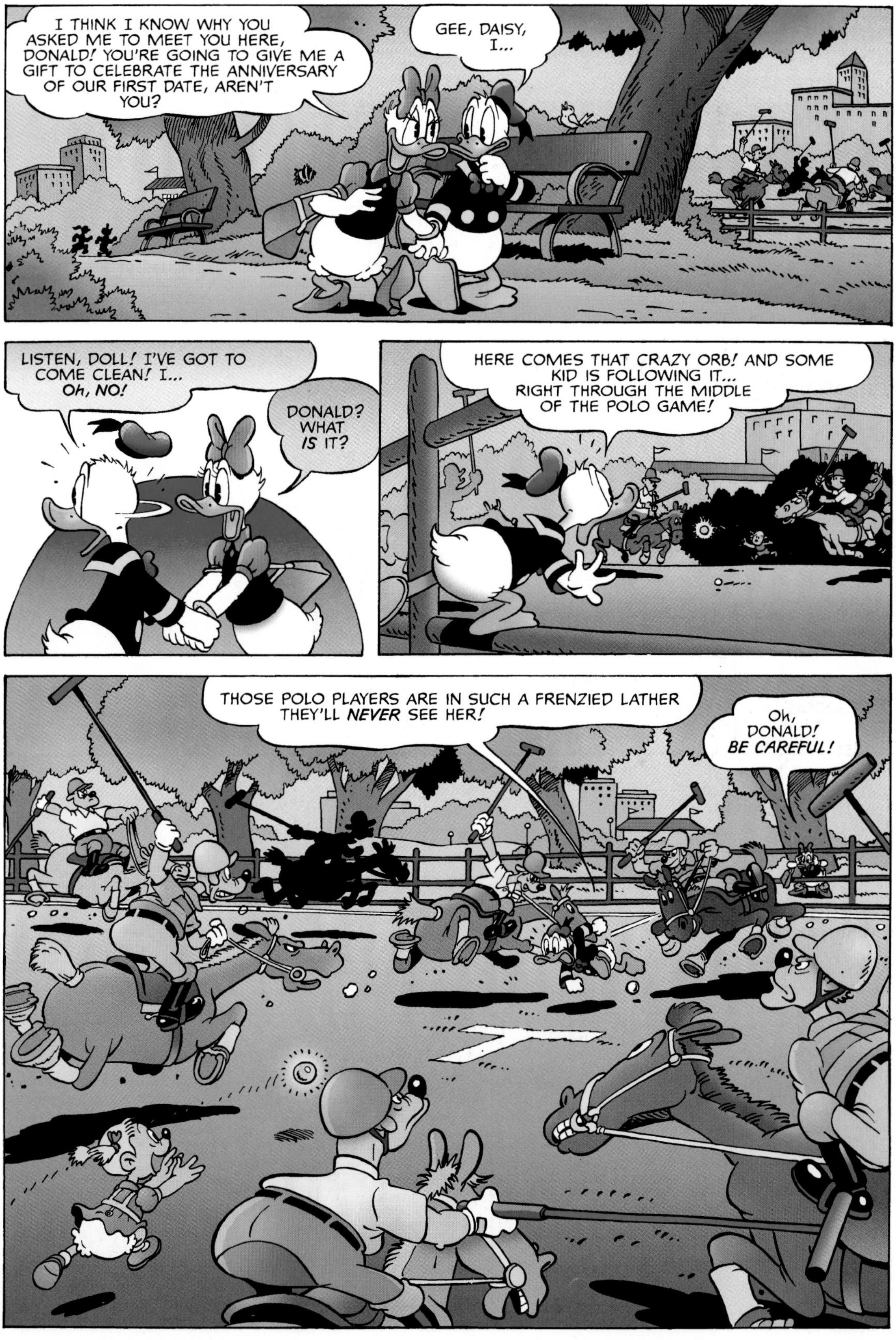
I THINK I KNOW WHY YOU ASKED ME TO MEET YOU HERE, DONALD! YOU'RE GOING TO GIVE ME A GIFT TO CELEBRATE THE ANNIVERSARY OF OUR FIRST DATE, AREN'T YOU?
GEE, DAISY, I...
LISTEN, DOLL! I'VE GOT TO COME CLEAN! I... *Oh, NO!*
DONALD? WHAT *IS* IT?
HERE COMES THAT CRAZY ORB! AND SOME KID IS FOLLOWING IT... RIGHT THROUGH THE MIDDLE OF THE POLO GAME!
THOSE POLO PLAYERS ARE IN SUCH A FRENZIED LATHER THEY'LL *NEVER* SEE HER!
Oh, DONALD! *BE CAREFUL!*

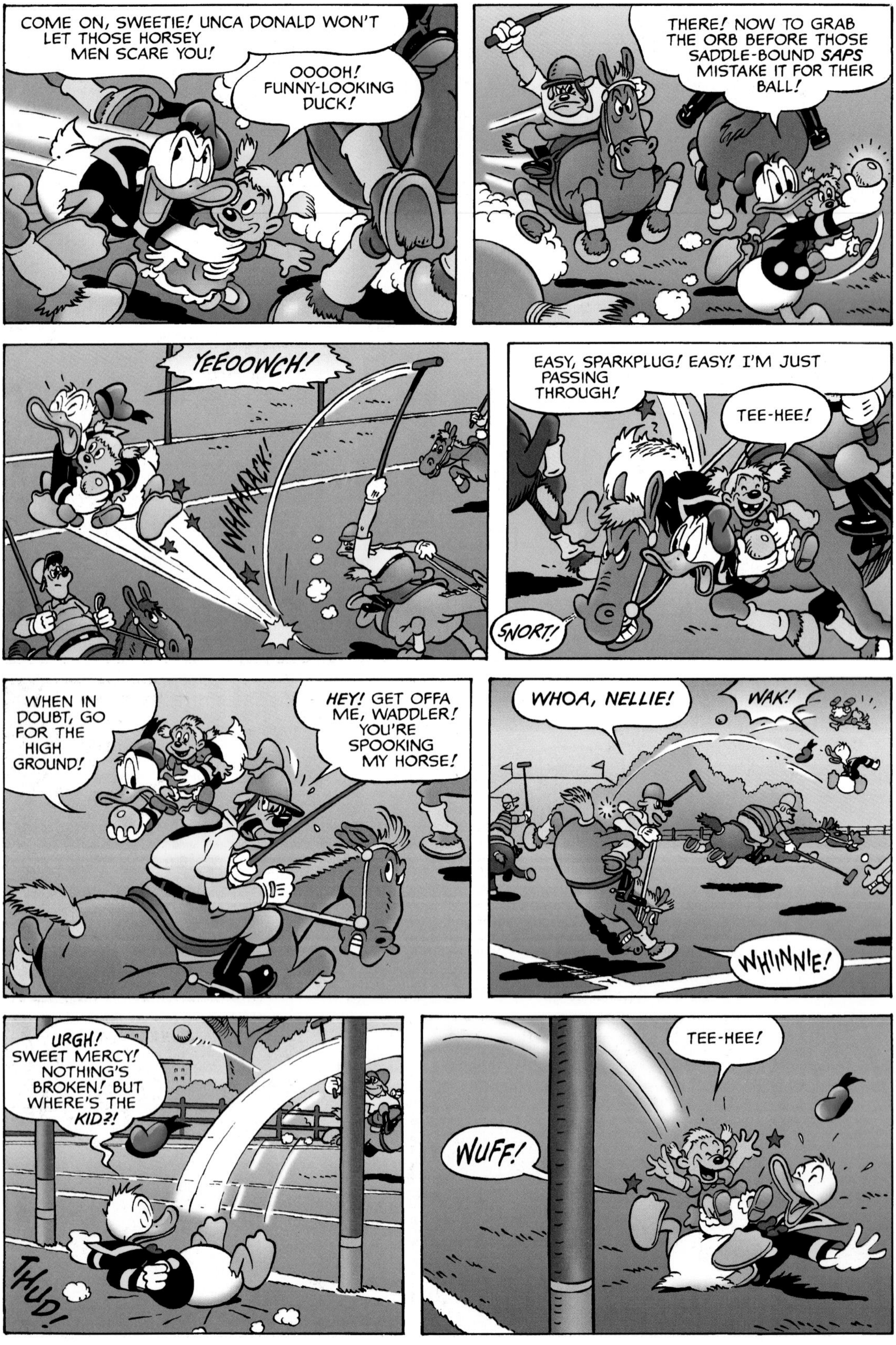
COME ON, SWEETIE! UNCA DONALD WON'T LET THOSE HORSEY MEN SCARE YOU!
OOOOH! FUNNY-LOOKING DUCK!
THERE! NOW TO GRAB THE ORB BEFORE THOSE SADDLE-BOUND SAPS MISTAKE IT FOR THEIR BALL!
YEEOOWCH!
WHAAACK!
EASY, SPARKPLUG! EASY! I'M JUST PASSING THROUGH!
TEE-HEE!
SNORT!
WHEN IN DOUBT, GO FOR THE HIGH GROUND!
HEY! GET OFFA ME, WADDLER! YOU'RE SPOOKING MY HORSE!
WHOA, NELLIE!
WAK!
WHINNIE!
URGH! SWEET MERCY! NOTHING'S BROKEN! BUT WHERE'S THE KID?!
THUD!
TEE-HEE!
WUFF!

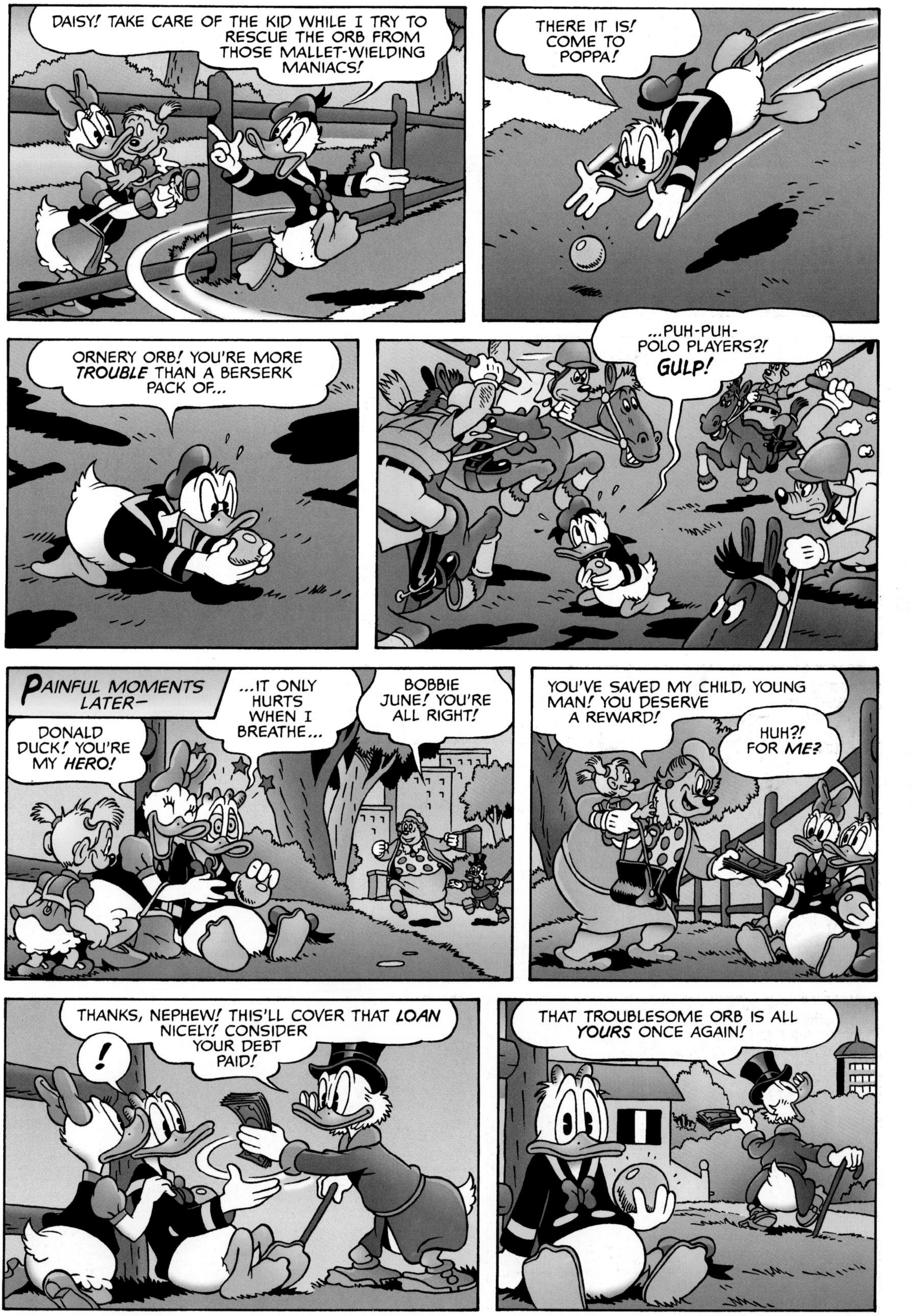
DAISY! TAKE CARE OF THE KID WHILE I TRY TO RESCUE THE ORB FROM THOSE MALLET-WIELDING MANIACS!
THERE IT IS! COME TO POPPA!
ORNERY ORB! YOU'RE MORE TROUBLE THAN A BERSERK PACK OF...
...PUH-PUH-POLO PLAYERS?! GULP!
PAINFUL MOMENTS LATER—
DONALD DUCK! YOU'RE MY HERO!
...IT ONLY HURTS WHEN I BREATHE...
BOBBIE JUNE! YOU'RE ALL RIGHT!
YOU'VE SAVED MY CHILD, YOUNG MAN! YOU DESERVE A REWARD!
HUH?! FOR ME?
!
THANKS, NEPHEW! THIS'LL COVER THAT LOAN NICELY! CONSIDER YOUR DEBT PAID!
THAT TROUBLESOME ORB IS ALL YOURS ONCE AGAIN!

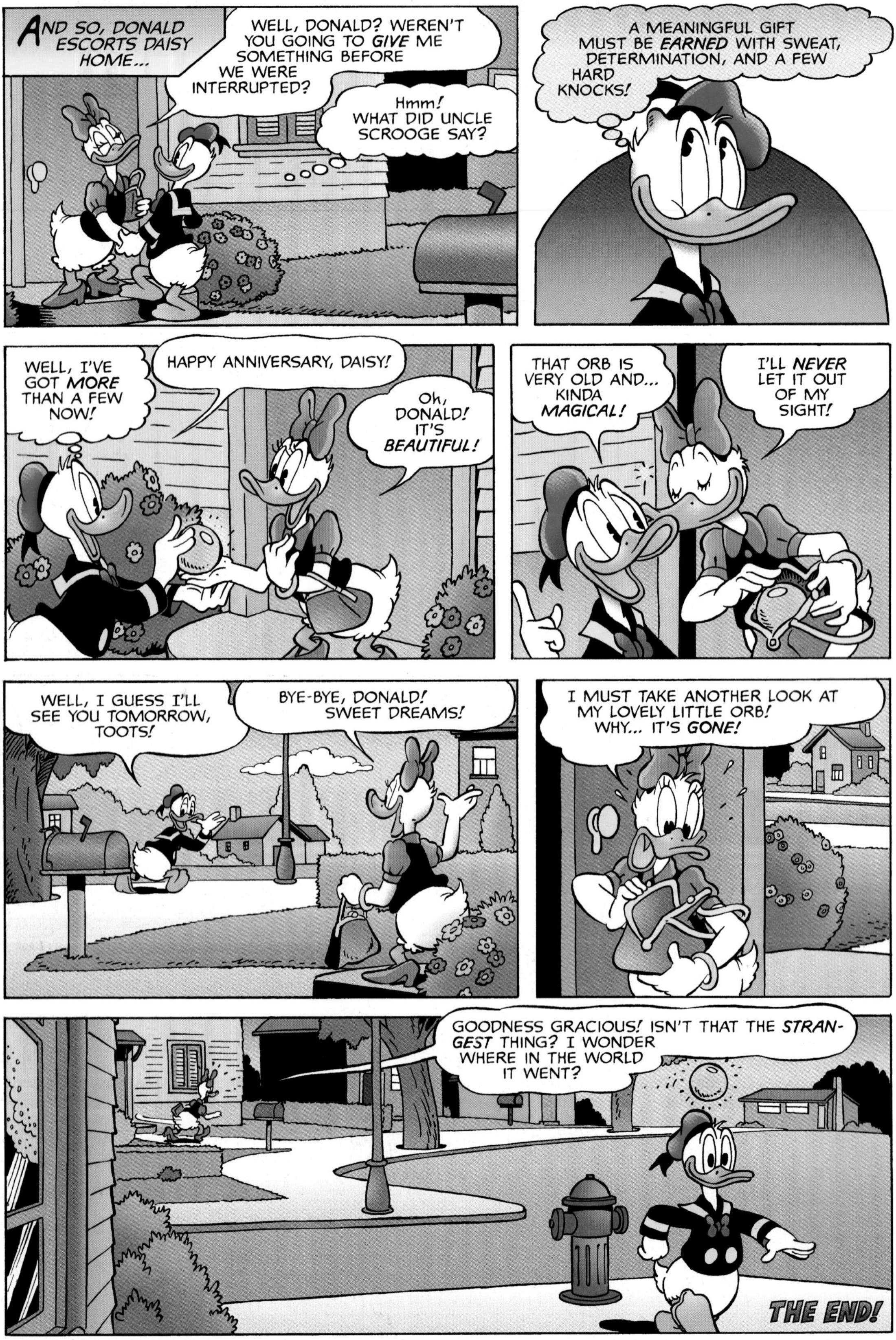
AND SO, DONALD ESCORTS DAISY HOME...
WELL, DONALD? WEREN'T YOU GOING TO GIVE ME SOMETHING BEFORE WE WERE INTERRUPTED?
Hmm! WHAT DID UNCLE SCROOGE SAY?
A MEANINGFUL GIFT MUST BE EARNED WITH SWEAT, DETERMINATION, AND A FEW HARD KNOCKS!
WELL, I'VE GOT MORE THAN A FEW NOW!
HAPPY ANNIVERSARY, DAISY!
Oh, DONALD! IT'S BEAUTIFUL!
THAT ORB IS VERY OLD AND... KINDA MAGICAL!
I'LL NEVER LET IT OUT OF MY SIGHT!
WELL, I GUESS I'LL SEE YOU TOMORROW, TOOTS!
BYE-BYE, DONALD! SWEET DREAMS!
I MUST TAKE ANOTHER LOOK AT MY LOVELY LITTLE ORB! WHY... IT'S GONE!
GOODNESS GRACIOUS! ISN'T THAT THE STRANGEST THING? I WONDER WHERE IN THE WORLD IT WENT?
THE END!

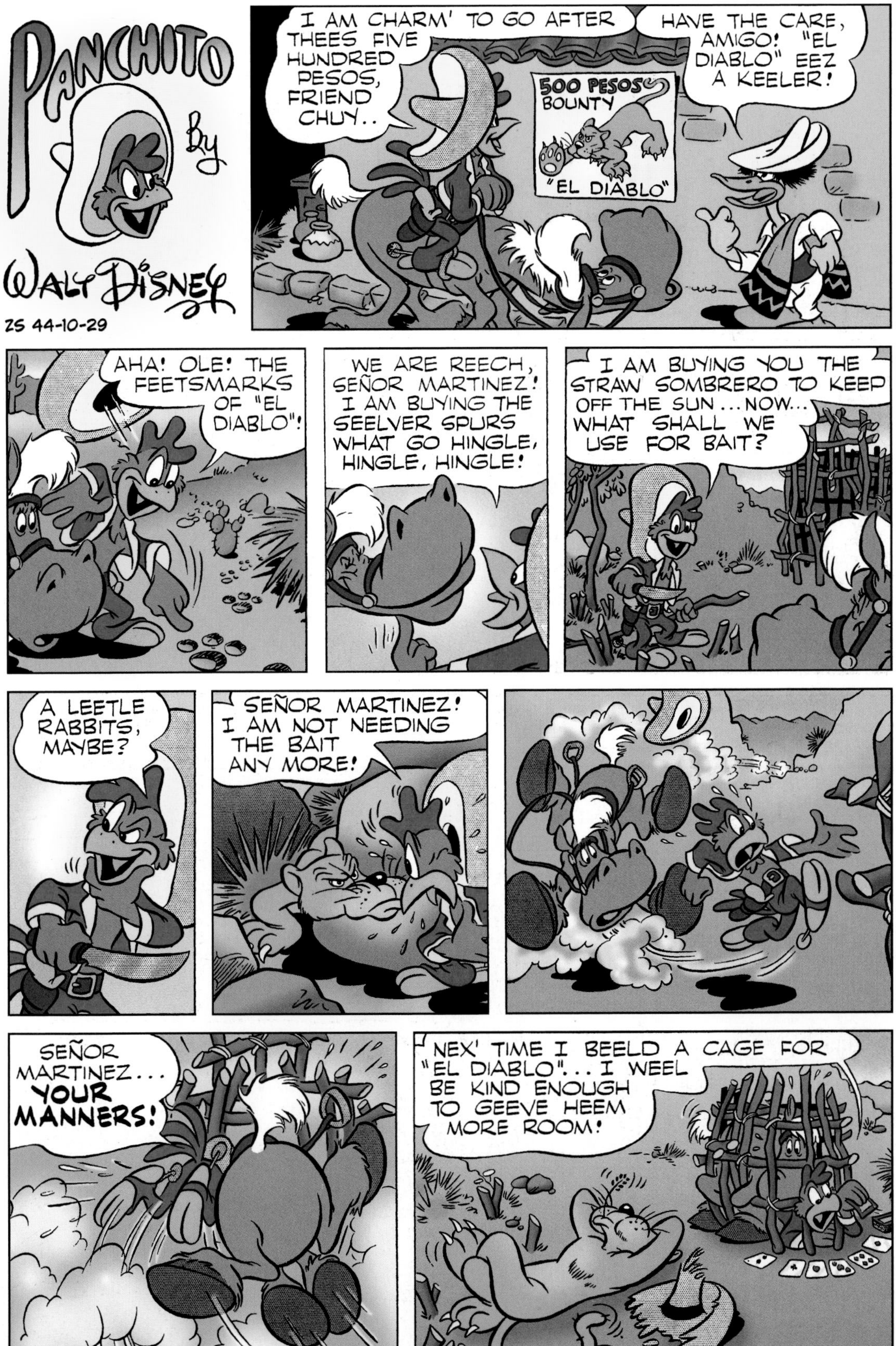

PANCHITO
By
WALT DISNEY
ZS 44-10-29
I AM CHARM' TO GO AFTER THEES FIVE HUNDRED PESOS, FRIEND CHUY..
500 PESOS BOUNTY
"EL DIABLO"
HAVE THE CARE, AMIGO! "EL DIABLO" EEZ A KEELER!
AHA! OLE! THE FEETSMARKS OF "EL DIABLO"!
WE ARE REECH, SEÑOR MARTINEZ! I AM BUYING THE SEELVER SPURS WHAT GO HINGLE, HINGLE, HINGLE!
I AM BUYING YOU THE STRAW SOMBRERO TO KEEP OFF THE SUN ... NOW... WHAT SHALL WE USE FOR BAIT?
A LEETLE RABBITS, MAYBE?
SEÑOR MARTINEZ! I AM NOT NEEDING THE BAIT ANY MORE!
SEÑOR MARTINEZ... YOUR MANNERS!
NEX' TIME I BEELD A CAGE FOR "EL DIABLO"... I WEEL BE KIND ENOUGH TO GEEVE HEEM MORE ROOM!

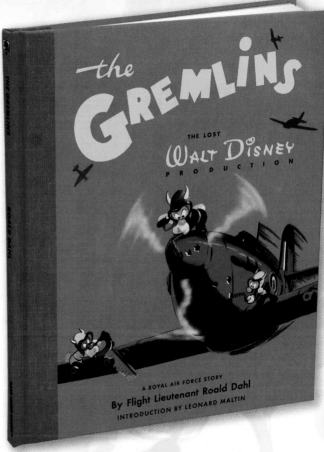

Walt Disney's Daisy Duck & Minnie Mouse in Sister Sleuths

PART 4 OF THE ORB SAGA

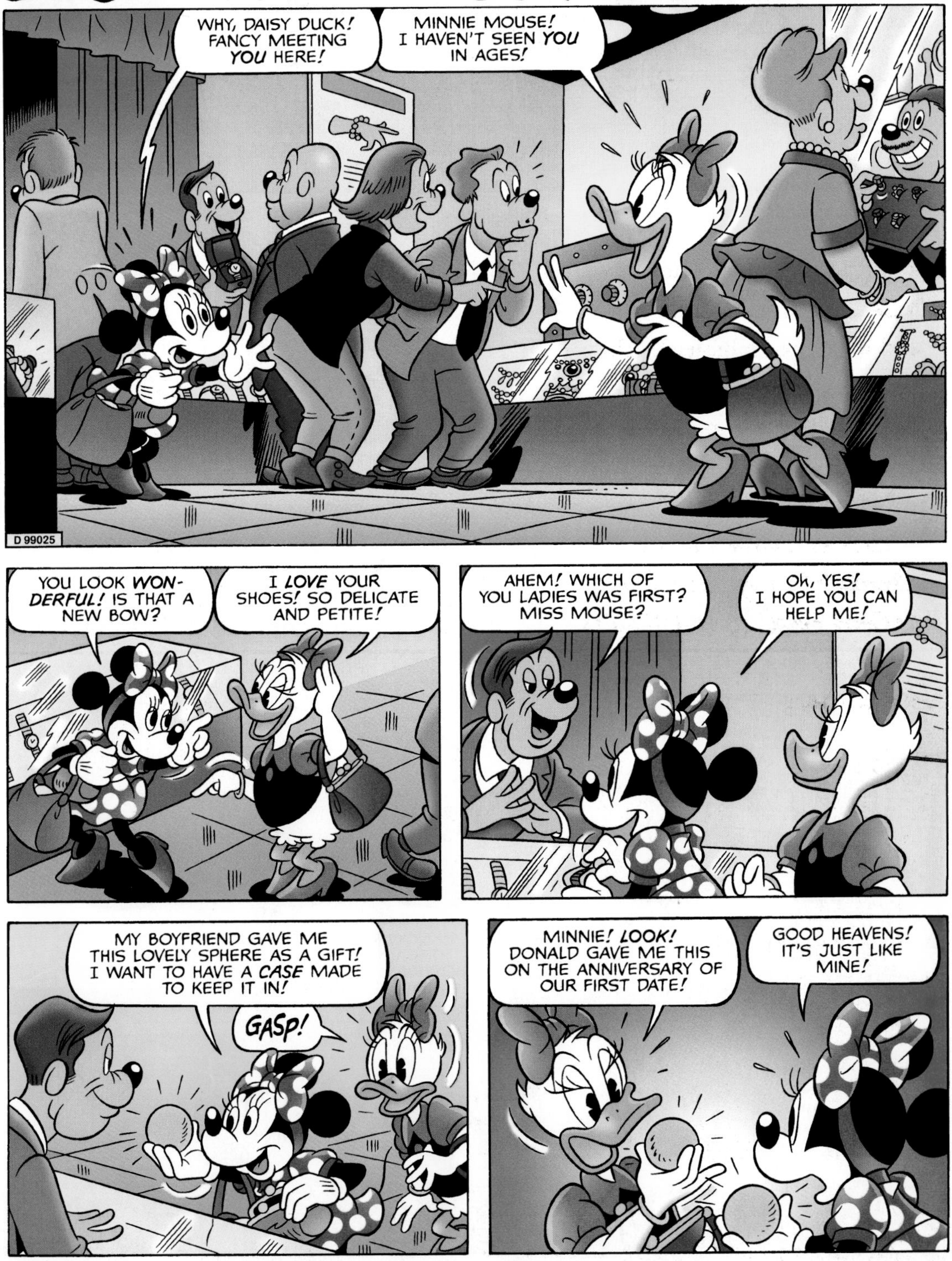
WHY, DAISY DUCK! FANCY MEETING YOU HERE!
MINNIE MOUSE! I HAVEN'T SEEN YOU IN AGES!
D 99025
YOU LOOK WONDERFUL! IS THAT A NEW BOW?
I LOVE YOUR SHOES! SO DELICATE AND PETITE!
AHEM! WHICH OF YOU LADIES WAS FIRST? MISS MOUSE?
Oh, YES! I HOPE YOU CAN HELP ME!
MY BOYFRIEND GAVE ME THIS LOVELY SPHERE AS A GIFT! I WANT TO HAVE A CASE MADE TO KEEP IT IN!
GASP!
MINNIE! LOOK! DONALD GAVE ME THIS ON THE ANNIVERSARY OF OUR FIRST DATE!
GOOD HEAVENS! IT'S JUST LIKE MINE!

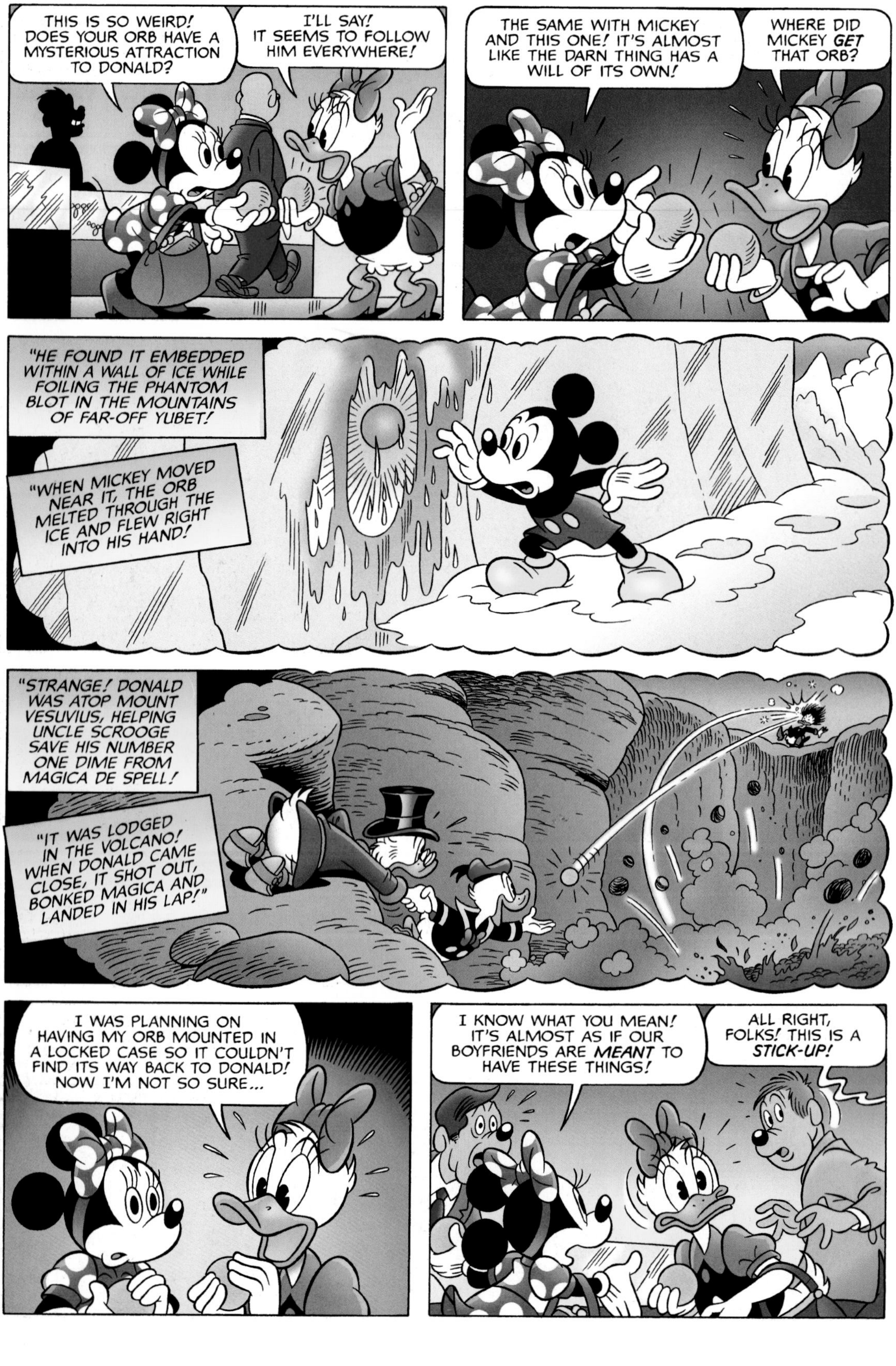
THIS IS SO WEIRD! DOES YOUR ORB HAVE A MYSTERIOUS ATTRACTION TO DONALD?
I'LL SAY! IT SEEMS TO FOLLOW HIM EVERYWHERE!
THE SAME WITH MICKEY AND THIS ONE! IT'S ALMOST LIKE THE DARN THING HAS A WILL OF ITS OWN!
WHERE DID MICKEY GET THAT ORB?
"HE FOUND IT EMBEDDED WITHIN A WALL OF ICE WHILE FOILING THE PHANTOM BLOT IN THE MOUNTAINS OF FAR-OFF YUBET!
"WHEN MICKEY MOVED NEAR IT, THE ORB MELTED THROUGH THE ICE AND FLEW RIGHT INTO HIS HAND!
"STRANGE! DONALD WAS ATOP MOUNT VESUVIUS, HELPING UNCLE SCROOGE SAVE HIS NUMBER ONE DIME FROM MAGICA DE SPELL!
"IT WAS LODGED IN THE VOLCANO! WHEN DONALD CAME CLOSE, IT SHOT OUT, BONKED MAGICA AND LANDED IN HIS LAP!"
I WAS PLANNING ON HAVING MY ORB MOUNTED IN A LOCKED CASE SO IT COULDN'T FIND ITS WAY BACK TO DONALD! NOW I'M NOT SO SURE...
I KNOW WHAT YOU MEAN! IT'S ALMOST AS IF OUR BOYFRIENDS ARE MEANT TO HAVE THESE THINGS!
ALL RIGHT, FOLKS! THIS IS A STICK-UP!

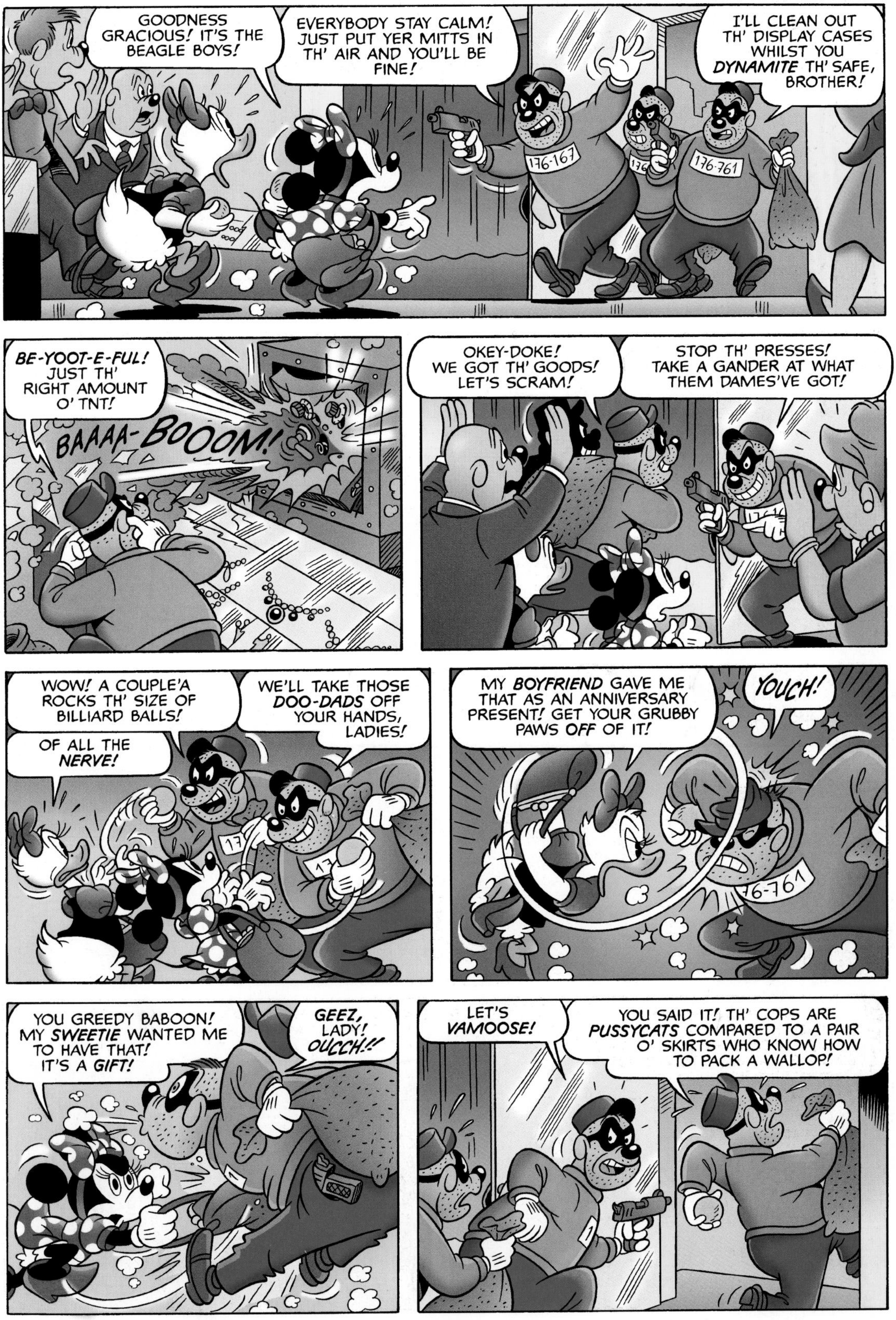
GOODNESS GRACIOUS! IT'S THE BEAGLE BOYS!
EVERYBODY STAY CALM! JUST PUT YER MITTS IN TH' AIR AND YOU'LL BE FINE!
I'LL CLEAN OUT TH' DISPLAY CASES WHILST YOU DYNAMITE TH' SAFE, BROTHER!
176-167
176-761
BE-YOOT-E-FUL! JUST TH' RIGHT AMOUNT O' TNT!
BAAAA-BOOOM!
OKEY-DOKE! WE GOT TH' GOODS! LET'S SCRAM!
STOP TH' PRESSES! TAKE A GANDER AT WHAT THEM DAMES'VE GOT!
WOW! A COUPLE'A ROCKS TH' SIZE OF BILLIARD BALLS!
WE'LL TAKE THOSE DOO-DADS OFF YOUR HANDS, LADIES!
OF ALL THE NERVE!
MY BOYFRIEND GAVE ME THAT AS AN ANNIVERSARY PRESENT! GET YOUR GRUBBY PAWS OFF OF IT!
YOUCH!
YOU GREEDY BABOON! MY SWEETIE WANTED ME TO HAVE THAT! IT'S A GIFT!
GEEZ, LADY! OUCCH!!
LET'S VAMOOSE!
YOU SAID IT! TH' COPS ARE PUSSYCATS COMPARED TO A PAIR O' SKIRTS WHO KNOW HOW TO PACK A WALLOP!

THOSE SLEAZY LOWLIFES CAN'T GET AWAY WITH THIS, MINNIE! I'LL FIND THEM IF IT'S THE *LAST* THING I DO!

I'M WITH YOU, SISTER! BUT WHERE DO WE LOOK?

I DON'T KNOW! MAYBE THEY LEFT A *CLUE* BEHIND!

HERE'S THE BOOK OF *MATCHES* THOSE STUMBLE-BUMS USED TO LIGHT THE DYNAMITE!

THE SLIMY SEAGULL?! THAT WHARFSIDE TAVERN IS AN UNDERWORLD HANGOUT! Hmmm...

WHAT'RE WE WAITING FOR? LET'S *GO!*

HOLD IT, DAISY! IT COULD BE A ROUGH JOINT! NOW WHAT IF WE WERE TO... PSSST... PSSST...

WHY, MINNIE! THAT'S A SIMPLY *WONDERFUL* IDEA!

THAT NIGHT—

The SLIMY SEAGULL

THIS DIVE IS FULL OF UNSAVORY CHARACTERS AND MUSCLE-BOUND BRUTES, DAISY! REMEMBER... ACT *TOUGH!*

Oh, DEAR!

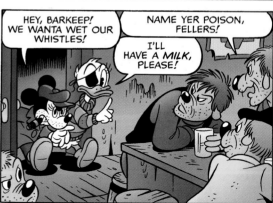

HEY, BARKEEP! WE WANTA WET OUR WHISTLES!

NAME YER POISON, FELLERS!

I'LL HAVE A *MILK*, PLEASE!

MILK?!

...Uh...

IN A *DIRTY* GLASS! AND MAKE IT *SNAPPY!*

YUH-YUH-YES, SIR!

ME 'N MY PARTNER ARE LOOKING FOR THREE SLEAZY WEASELS BY THE NAME O' THE BEAGLE BOYS!

AN' JUST WHY ARE YOU PIPSQUEAKS SO INTERESTED IN THEIR WHEREABOUTS?

WE HEAR THEY GOT SOME LOOT TO FENCE!

WHUMP!

AN' WE'RE THE BEST FENCES IN TOWN! ANYONE GOT A PROBLEM WITH THAT?!

NUH-NUH-NO, SIR!

YEAH, I SEEN THEM GUYS! THEY HANG OUT IN HERE SOMETIMES! SO WHAT?!

SO WE'LL PAY TOP DOLLAR FOR THEIR LOOT! THAT'S WHAT!!

KAA-RAASH!

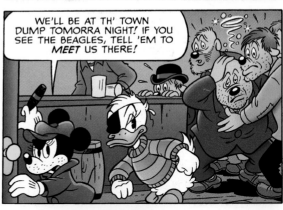

WE'LL BE AT TH' TOWN DUMP TOMORRA NIGHT! IF YOU SEE THE BEAGLES, TELL 'EM TO MEET US THERE!

TEE-HEE! ACTING TOUGH ISN'T SO TOUGH, AFTER ALL! IN FACT, IT'S A LOT OF FUN!

WHY, DAISY DUCK! AT LAST I UNDERSTAND HOW YOU MANAGE TO KEEP DONALD IN LINE!

The SLIMY SEAGULL

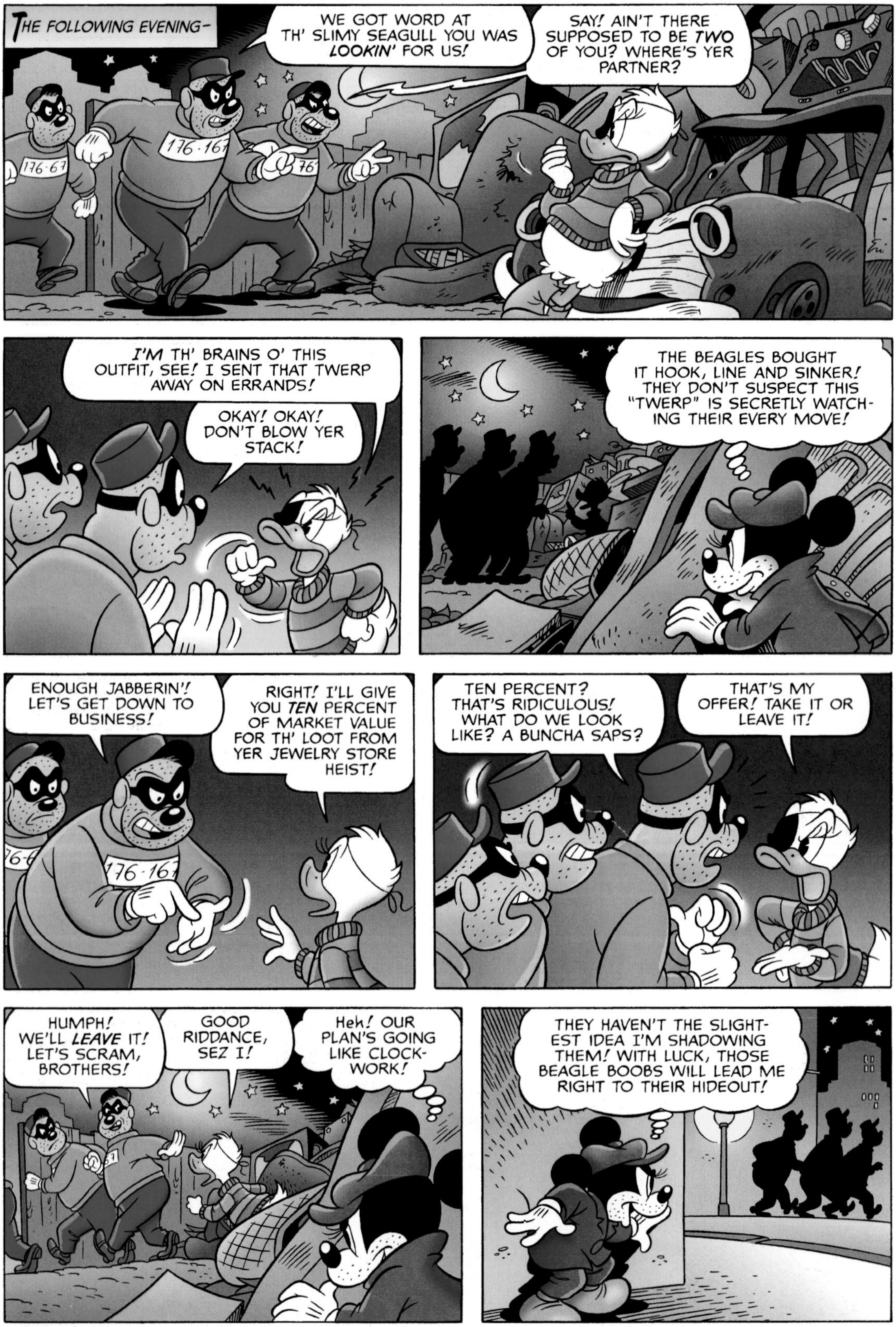
THE FOLLOWING EVENING—
WE GOT WORD AT TH' SLIMY SEAGULL YOU WAS LOOKIN' FOR US!
SAY! AIN'T THERE SUPPOSED TO BE TWO OF YOU? WHERE'S YER PARTNER?
176-167
176-67
I'M TH' BRAINS O' THIS OUTFIT, SEE! I SENT THAT TWERP AWAY ON ERRANDS!
OKAY! OKAY! DON'T BLOW YER STACK!
THE BEAGLES BOUGHT IT HOOK, LINE AND SINKER! THEY DON'T SUSPECT THIS "TWERP" IS SECRETLY WATCHING THEIR EVERY MOVE!
ENOUGH JABBERIN'! LET'S GET DOWN TO BUSINESS!
RIGHT! I'LL GIVE YOU TEN PERCENT OF MARKET VALUE FOR TH' LOOT FROM YER JEWELRY STORE HEIST!
TEN PERCENT? THAT'S RIDICULOUS! WHAT DO WE LOOK LIKE? A BUNCHA SAPS?
THAT'S MY OFFER! TAKE IT OR LEAVE IT!
HUMPH! WE'LL LEAVE IT! LET'S SCRAM, BROTHERS!
GOOD RIDDANCE, SEZ I!
Heh! OUR PLAN'S GOING LIKE CLOCKWORK!
THEY HAVEN'T THE SLIGHTEST IDEA I'M SHADOWING THEM! WITH LUCK, THOSE BEAGLE BOOBS WILL LEAD ME RIGHT TO THEIR HIDEOUT!

BRIGHT AND EARLY THE NEXT MORNING—

WELL, MINNIE, THANKS TO YOUR PLAN, WE KNOW WHERE THOSE CREEPS ARE HOLED UP!

NOW WE JUST WAIT FOR THEM TO GO OUT FOR THE DAY!

SHORTLY—

COME ON, BOYS! LET'S LEAVE TH' LOOT IN THE HIDEOUT AND FIND US A FENCE WHO'LL GIVE US A SQUARE DEAL!

YEAH! WE NEED A FENCE WHO AIN'T *CROOKED!*

THIS SHOULDN'T TAKE LONG! WE'LL SIMPLY NAB OUR ORBS AND SKE-DADDLE!

DRAT! THOSE RASCALS LOCKED THE DOOR! DO YOU HAVE A HAIRPIN, DAISY?

UGH! WHAT POOR HOUSEKEEPERS! HOW ARE WE SUPPOSED TO FIND *ANYTHING* IN THIS MESS?

I GUESS WE JUST START LOOKING!

LONG MINUTES LATER—

I HAVEN'T TURNED UP A THING! HOW ABOUT YOU? ANY LUCK?

ONLY IF YOU CALL UNWASHED SOCKS LUCKY!

AHA! A WALL SAFE! NO DOUBT OUR ORBS AND THE JEWELS ARE IN THERE!

I DON'T THINK YOU CAN OPEN *THAT* WITH A HAIR PIN!

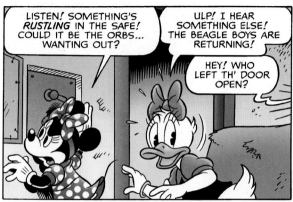

LISTEN! SOMETHING'S *RUSTLING* IN THE SAFE! COULD IT BE THE ORBS... WANTING OUT?

ULP! I HEAR SOMETHING ELSE! THE BEAGLE BOYS ARE RETURNING!

HEY! WHO LEFT TH' DOOR OPEN?

BEHIND THE DRAPES, DAISY! *QUICKLY!*

YOU DON'T HAVE TO TELL ME TWICE, SISTER!

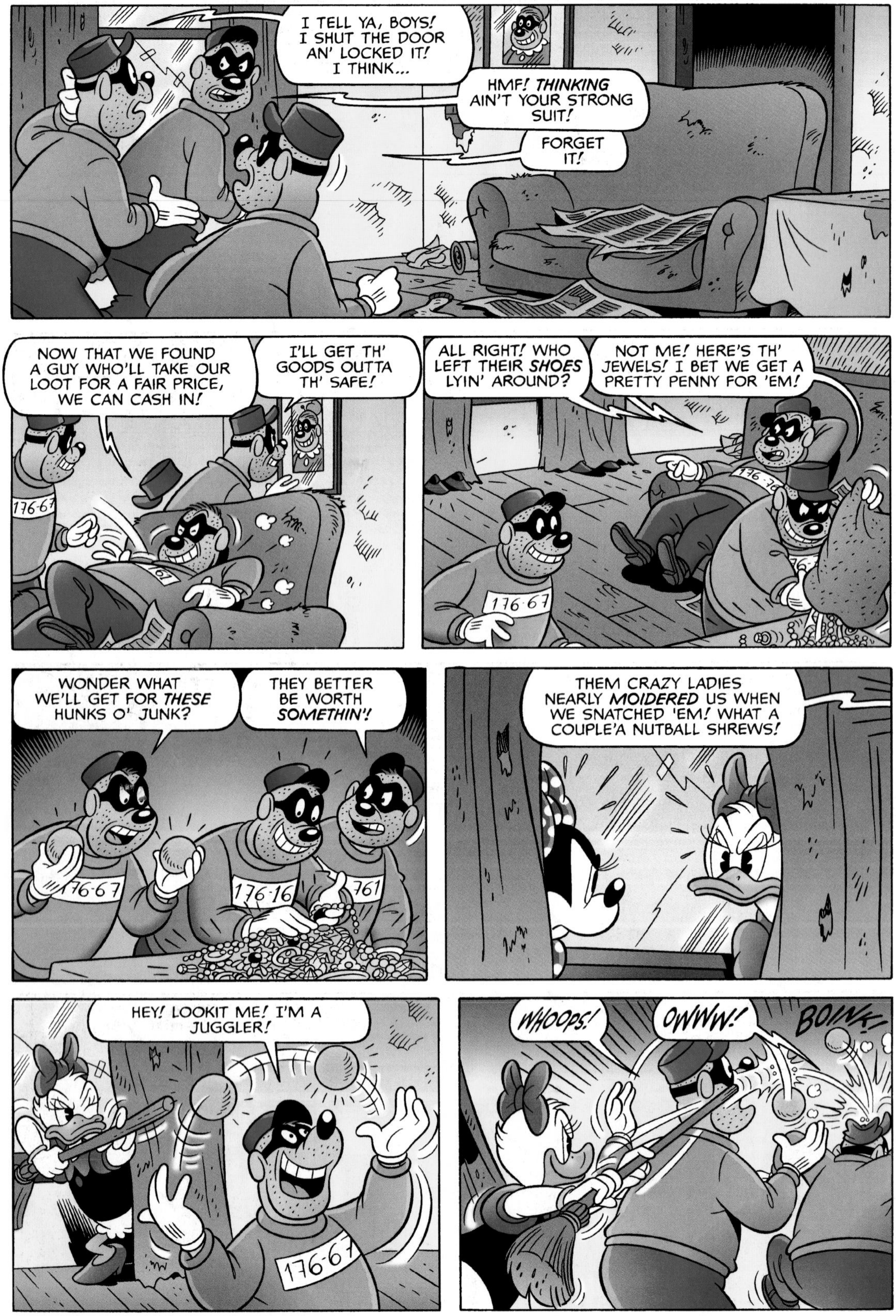
I TELL YA, BOYS! I SHUT THE DOOR AN' LOCKED IT! I THINK...
HMF! THINKING AIN'T YOUR STRONG SUIT!
FORGET IT!
NOW THAT WE FOUND A GUY WHO'LL TAKE OUR LOOT FOR A FAIR PRICE, WE CAN CASH IN!
I'LL GET TH' GOODS OUTTA TH' SAFE!
176-67
ALL RIGHT! WHO LEFT THEIR SHOES LYIN' AROUND?
NOT ME! HERE'S TH' JEWELS! I BET WE GET A PRETTY PENNY FOR 'EM!
176-67
WONDER WHAT WE'LL GET FOR THESE HUNKS O' JUNK?
THEY BETTER BE WORTH SOMETHIN'!
176-67
176-16
761
THEM CRAZY LADIES NEARLY MOIDERED US WHEN WE SNATCHED 'EM! WHAT A COUPLE'A NUTBALL SHREWS!
HEY! LOOKIT ME! I'M A JUGGLER!
176-67
WHOOPS!
OWWW!
BOINK!

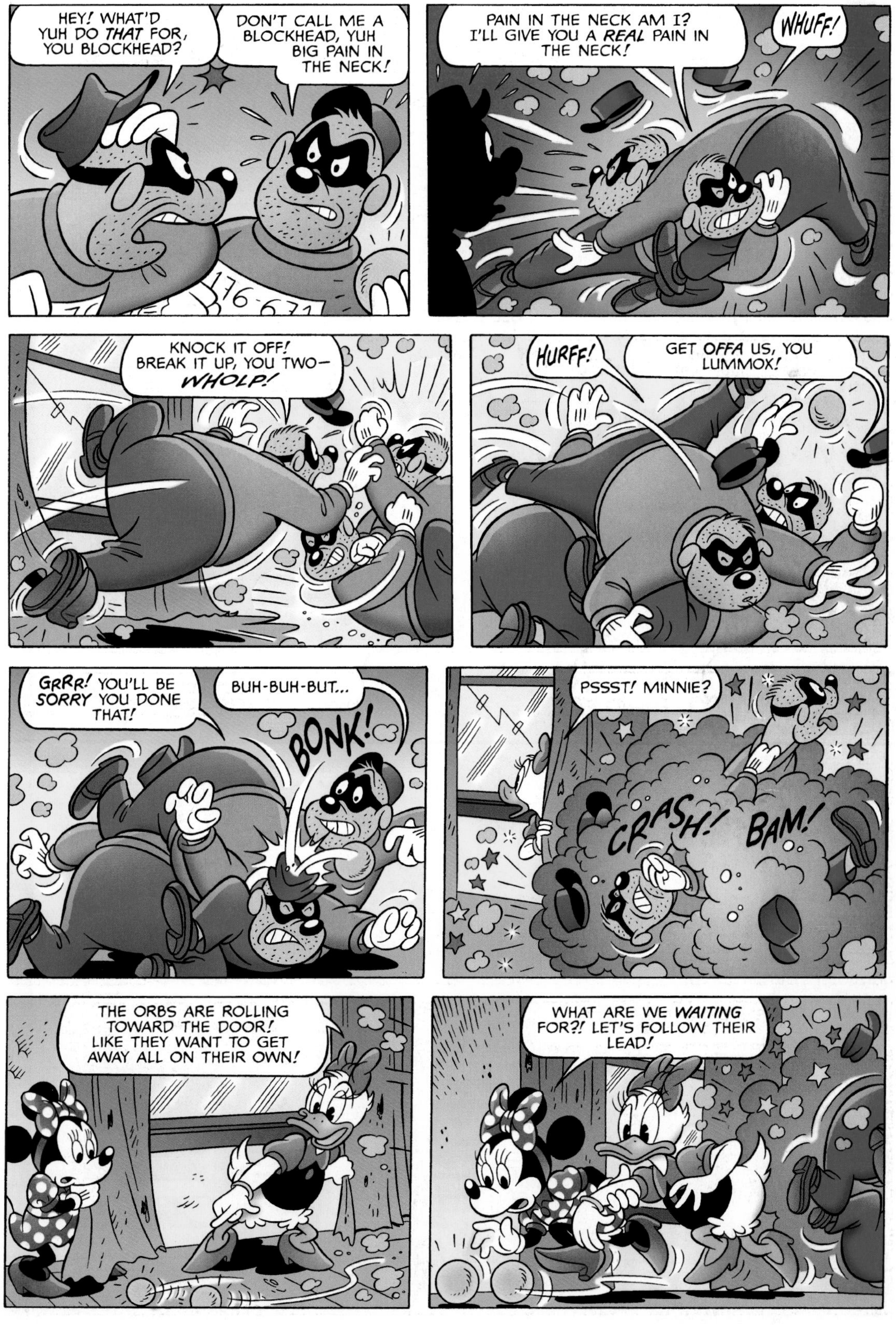
HEY! WHAT'D YUH DO THAT FOR, YOU BLOCKHEAD?
DON'T CALL ME A BLOCKHEAD, YUH BIG PAIN IN THE NECK!
PAIN IN THE NECK AM I? I'LL GIVE YOU A REAL PAIN IN THE NECK!
WHUFF!
KNOCK IT OFF! BREAK IT UP, YOU TWO— WHOLP!
HURFF!
GET OFFA US, YOU LUMMOX!
GRRR! YOU'LL BE SORRY YOU DONE THAT!
BUH-BUH-BUT...
BONK!
PSSST! MINNIE?
CRASH! BAM!
THE ORBS ARE ROLLING TOWARD THE DOOR! LIKE THEY WANT TO GET AWAY ALL ON THEIR OWN!
WHAT ARE WE WAITING FOR?! LET'S FOLLOW THEIR LEAD!

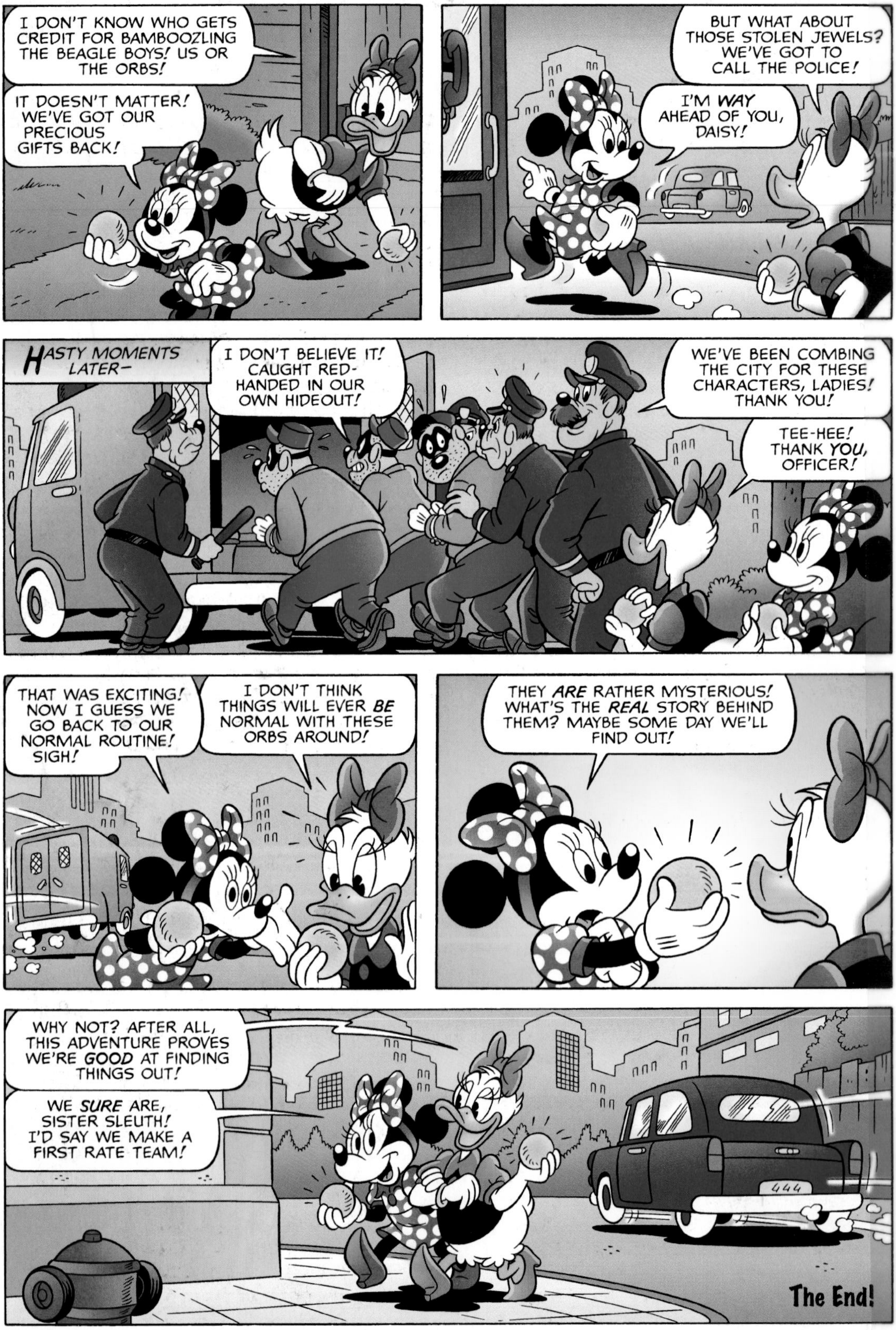
I DON'T KNOW WHO GETS CREDIT FOR BAMBOOZLING THE BEAGLE BOYS! US OR THE ORBS!
IT DOESN'T MATTER! WE'VE GOT OUR PRECIOUS GIFTS BACK!
BUT WHAT ABOUT THOSE STOLEN JEWELS? WE'VE GOT TO CALL THE POLICE!
I'M WAY AHEAD OF YOU, DAISY!
HASTY MOMENTS LATER—
I DON'T BELIEVE IT! CAUGHT RED-HANDED IN OUR OWN HIDEOUT!
WE'VE BEEN COMBING THE CITY FOR THESE CHARACTERS, LADIES! THANK YOU!
TEE-HEE! THANK YOU, OFFICER!
THAT WAS EXCITING! NOW I GUESS WE GO BACK TO OUR NORMAL ROUTINE! SIGH!
I DON'T THINK THINGS WILL EVER BE NORMAL WITH THESE ORBS AROUND!
THEY ARE RATHER MYSTERIOUS! WHAT'S THE REAL STORY BEHIND THEM? MAYBE SOME DAY WE'LL FIND OUT!
WHY NOT? AFTER ALL, THIS ADVENTURE PROVES WE'RE GOOD AT FINDING THINGS OUT!
WE SURE ARE, SISTER SLEUTH! I'D SAY WE MAKE A FIRST RATE TEAM!
The End!